ANNE

THE PRIVATE PRINCESS REVEALED

In this biography of the Princess Royal, Brian Hoey, who has known her for more than twenty-five years, tells the story of her life and work today. He describes how she survived the trauma of the break-up of her first marriage to Mark Phillips and succeeded in persuading her family to accept Tim Laurence as her new husband. He has talked to her closest personal friends, such as Andrew Parker Bowles and Malcolm Wallace, two men who have known her since she was a rebellious teenager and seen her mature into the caring, hard-working Princess she is today. James Beaton, the Princess's personal bodyguard, speaks out about what exactly it was like to be involved in her attempted kidnapping. And Hoey also tells the story of her annual Christmas party, which is attended by her ex-husband, but not the current one. And there is much more in this revealing and readable book.

ANNE

The Private Princess Revealed .

Brian Hoey

CHIVERS PRESS
BATH

First published 1997
by
Sidgwick & Jackson
This Large Print edition published by
Chivers Press
by arrangement with
Macmillan Publishers Ltd
1999

ISBN 0 7540 1253 0

British Library Cataloguing in Publication Data available

Printed and bound in Great Britain by
REDWOOD BOOKS, Trowbridge, Wiltshire

CONTENTS

Introduction
In Search of the Princess vii

1 The Princess Royal 1

2 The Formative Years 12

3 Anne and Mark 23

4 Gunfire on The Mall 37

5 A Very Civilized Divorce 62

6 Two Weddings 77

7 Tim Laurence 90

8 Gatcombe Park 110

9 Friends and Neighbours 121

10 Peter and Zara—Family Life 142

11 World Traveller 153

12 The Office 171

13 The Princess and the Press 198

14 Celebrity Pals 218

15 A Competitive Horsewoman 221

16 President Anne? 242

17 A Future Role? 254

Appendix
Holders of the Title The Princess Royal 265

INTRODUCTION

IN SEARCH OF THE PRINCESS

Princess Anne is one of the most complex and frequently misunderstood members of what has been described as the ultimate dysfunctional family. She has carried on a series of running battles with the world's media for most of her adult life, even when they have tried to be kind to her. A self-admitted workaholic, she refuses to allow her children to have titles, but accepted for herself the title of Princess Royal and style of Knight of the Garter, and has emerged as the most respected and hard-working Royal of her generation, seen by many as the possible saviour of the Monarchy. She has survived the trauma of a marriage break-up in the full glare of national publicity, and successfully, and seamlessly, contracted a second marriage—to one of her mother's former servants.

I have known her since she first burst on to the international sporting stage at the age of twenty-one, when I was a reporter working for BBC Television News. I had been sent to interview her as she tried to win the European Three-Day Event title—which she did at her first attempt. After being introduced by her then close friend, Richard Meade, and following the interview—which was transmitted all over the world—I was invited to a private lunch at Buckingham Palace.

Just before Princess Anne became engaged to Mark Phillips, in 1973, I was despatched to Balmoral, along with a camera crew, to try to secure a 'scoop' interview. Her Royal Highness invited me into Craigowan, where Prince Charles and his then Equerry, Captain Nicholas Soames, were staying, having travelled from the West Indies, just for the weekend, in order to be present. I was privileged to be the first outsider to be told of the betrothal, and when offered a glass of sherry to toast the couple, found I was the only one drinking. I then had to travel overnight to London where the official announcement was to be made the following morning, and presented myself at Buckingham Palace just in time to film the engagement interview on the rear terrace, in company with the late Reginald Bosanquet of ITN.

Since that time I have become associated professionally with the Princess on a number of occasions, writing the first biography of her with her full cooperation in 1984, and then in 1989 a second book—again with her help and agreement—which was published on the day she announced her separation from Mark Phillips. During one of our overseas journeys—to Houston in Texas to raise funds for the British Olympic team—she was amused (I think) to hear herself described as 'the only woman in the world who travels with a personal biographer'.

I also spent the best part of a year in her company when Thames Television commissioned a documentary programme about her working life, for which we travelled the length and breadth of the United Kingdom, sometimes with her driving her Reliant Scimitar sports car (she now favours a Bentley Turbo), the car stereo blaring away at full volume. The Princess opened many doors for the television team. We filmed her at Buckingham

Palace and at Windsor, spent hours together at Gatcombe Park—with a short break while she gave birth to Zara—and were received as her guests at the Palace of Holyroodhouse in Edinburgh, where we were given a rare insight into life at the Scottish Court. She could not have been more professional or courteous, even when one of our party betrayed her trust and sold his 'inside story' to a tabloid newspaper.

With her permission I spoke to anyone I wanted to meet who I felt had something to contribute to her story. Her former headmistress, the late Miss Elizabeth Clarke, who had never before uttered a word in public about her Royal pupil, talked frankly and honestly about the problems in taking on the Sovereign's daughter. But, ever suspicious, she checked back with the Princess's office while I sat in her house in Kent, to make sure I was who I said I was, and that I really did have the Princess's permission to interview her. It was the same with all Princess Anne's friends, colleagues and staff. Once they were assured that I was the genuine article bearing the 'Royal seal of approval', they opened up completely.

When I was asked to write this latest book about the Princess Royal, I knew that it needed to say something new about her. After all, her earlier life had been comprehensively documented. She had had millions of words devoted to her in newspapers and magazines throughout the world. And as the first daughter of a reigning British Sovereign to be divorced and remarried she had already secured a dubious place in Royal history, even if her own divorce has been overshadowed by the acrimonious and very public break-up of the marriages of two of her brothers.

Then I realized that since her separation from Mark Phillips, no serious effort had been made to chronicle her current lifestyle. Nobody has written about the way she has coped with being a single parent—even if it was only for a matter of months—or how she arranged her second marriage to Tim Laurence. Details of the engagement were fuzzy, as were opinions on how Tim has fitted into the Gatcombe Set. The reaction of the people who were friends to both the Princess and Mark Phillips needed to be sought. I wanted to hear from authoritative sources what the future might hold for the Princess Royal—what, for instance, the divorce of the Prince and Princess of Wales could mean to her in terms of her future role within the Royal Family.

Tim Laurence is also something of a closed book. He comes from a background that could hardly have been further removed from that of his wife, and I felt it would be interesting to hear how he has become assimilated into the Royal Family and also whether he has retained friends from his previous non-Royal life.

The Princess herself was understandably less than enthusiastic when I broached the subject of yet another book. She and all the other members of the Royal Family are naturally suspicious of authors, particularly after the disasters of the Princess of Wales's apparent cooperation in a best-selling 'kiss-and-tell' book, followed closely by Prince Charles's decision to reveal all in a television programme and an authorized biography.

The Princess Royal had already given me her

views and comments on most subjects over a number of years and did not see the point in merely reiterating them (neither did I), but she did not raise too many serious objections when I said I would like to speak to several of her closest friends.

Perhaps the most important of these is Andrew Parker Bowles. He has known her for more than a quarter of a century, first as an early boyfriend and subsequently as a valued and much trusted confidant. So when he agreed to see me I knew I was going to hear views that were authentic and totally honest. This was not going to be one of those 'sources at Court' or 'a close friend' type of story. Everything Andrew Parker Bowles told me is in quotable and attributable form. And, like Elizabeth Clarke some years before, he also telephoned the Princess to check my bona fides. Once they had been established to his satisfaction he welcomed me to his home (Princess Anne actually telephoned him while I was there) and spoke with refreshing frankness about his personal and professional relationship with Her Royal Highness. Descriptions of dinner parties at Gatcombe, Tim Laurence's love of gardening and Peter and Zara Phillips's acceptance of their stepfather, could only have come from someone with an intimate knowledge of the family and I was delighted that Andrew Parker Bowles chose to entrust his unique information to me. Considering his own recent marital difficulties, with his high-profile divorce from the woman identified as the mistress of the Prince of Wales, it would have been perfectly understandable if he had run a mile when I approached him. But he didn't, and I am very grateful.

Similarly, Malcolm Wallace, another old friend of more than twenty years' standing, whose former wife is a Lady-in-Waiting to the Princess Royal, gave a revealing insight into Her Royal Highness's character when he told me how she comforted him after his wife walked out, taking their children with her. He also explained how his close relationship with Mark Phillips has meant distancing himself from the Princess these days: as he put it, 'Civilized behaviour only goes so far.'

Continuing the theme of the Princess Royal's home and working life, I spoke to the man who lends her his house every year so that she can give all her staff and their spouses a Christmas party, and found out that while Mark and the children attend, Tim does not—another facet of Royal life that has never been revealed before.

The man who suffered appalling injuries after being shot five times while trying to protect the Princess during the kidnapping attempt in The Mall, Chief Superintendent James Beaton, has also given exclusively his own first-hand account of the gun battle (see Chapter 4). Jim Beaton has never before spoken publicly about the incident, after which he was awarded the George Cross—the highest civilian award for bravery in this country—and later made a Commander of the Royal Victorian Order by a grateful Queen for his efforts to save her daughter. As the man with sole responsibility for Princess Anne's safety, he placed his own life in danger not once but five times during that ten-minute episode, and his account of the dramatic happenings of that night in 1974 bring to life one of the most traumatic experiences any member of the Royal Family has undergone.

The severe restrictions that are placed on all members of the Royal Household mean that they are forbidden to disclose any information about the Royal Family, or other members of the Household, at any time. So when I was also able to talk to a number of footmen, including one who had worked personally for Tim Laurence when he was an Equerry to the Queen, this was naturally done with a guarantee of confidentiality from me. If they were discovered it could have meant instant dismissal and possible prosecution.

The same applied to present and former officers and ratings in the Royal Navy, including several who had served with Tim Laurence on the Royal Yacht *Britannia*. They were prepared to give background information about him on condition that their names were not used, and I have respected their confidence on all occasions. The Governor of the Falkland Islands, Richard Ralph, who was not bound by the same conventions, spoke frankly to me about the Princess's first visit to his domain, revealing that 'she does the tiara stuff beautifully if necessary, but prefers the informality of jeans and anoraks'. Other residents of the Falklands gave me their completely unofficial impressions of their Royal visitor. As one of them, perhaps slightly tactlessly, put it, 'The Argies got Diana, we got Anne. There's no doubt that in Royal terms, we got the best of the bargain.'

Members of the Princess Royal's staff were able to brief me on how her working life has changed in recent years and on the difference that Tim Laurence has made in private to the Princess's outlook on life. I was told why he insisted on renting a London flat when they were first married, and also why and when they gave it up.

Carol Darby, who designed and made the Princess's engagement and wedding rings, let me in on the secret of how Tim Laurence approached her just a couple of weeks after Anne's divorce, to order the rings for a wedding that was to take place seven months later. She even provided me with her original drawings of the rings.

In 1992 the Princess was nominated for the Nobel Peace Prize for her work on famine relief in the Third World. I am able to publish for the first time the letter of nomination as submitted by Lord Callaghan of Cardiff and to name two of the world leaders who supported her nomination.

Perhaps the most significant episode in Princess Anne's life is yet to come. As her brother Charles prepares for his role as future King, Anne is being groomed by the Queen to take an increasingly important part in Royal affairs. With Charles apparently destined to remain single while he is on the throne, his sister is the obvious person to act as his consort. Having spoken to a number of senior courtiers about the prospect, I have been able to detail the arguments for and against the proposal. And I am able to open the debate on another contentious issue. If Britain were to become a republic, would the Princess Royal be the right choice as our first President?

Certain parts of this book have been verified for accuracy by those who have contributed to it, including members of the Royal Household, but there has been no attempt by the Princess Royal to exercise editorial control, or to have any part of it deleted. All opinions, other than those attributed to quotable sources, are mine and mine alone.

Furthermore, I hereby promise Her Royal Highness that this will be the last book I shall write about her. She has given me more help than any author has a right to expect, so from now on, Ma'am, I will leave you in peace.

Brian Hoey

CHAPTER ONE

THE PRINCESS ROYAL

Her Royal Highness, the Princess Anne Elizabeth Alice Louise, The Princess Royal, KG, GCVO, QSO, is not a woman to mess with, as numerous people have found to their cost. As the Queen's only daughter, she has never been anything other than Royal, and while she professes to care little about titles herself, she nevertheless has a very regal reaction to anyone careless enough to forget her status for a moment. Although there is no truth in the story that when a tabloid photographer asked her to 'look this way, love' she icily replied, 'I am not your love I am Your Royal Highness,' she has a certain awareness of her own position.

When the Queen elevated her daughter to be a Lady of Garter in 1994, the Princess was entitled to affix the letters LG after her name. Apparently this was not to her liking, for she asked Her Majesty, and was granted, permission to use the letters KG instead. KG signifies a Knight of the Garter, and she now has the Queen's consent to use those letters, which, in fact, makes her the only female KG in the world.

Because she takes part in horse-racing, Three-Day Eventing and sailing, and also appears in public more frequently than any other member of the Royal family, people occasionally labour under the misapprehension that the Princess Royal is more approachable than say, Prince Philip or Princess Margaret. Nothing could be further from the truth. She can be as distant and as proud as any of the others, and her down-to-earth approach to the problems she encounters in her role as President of the Save the Children Fund conceals a natural haughtiness, which perhaps also results from generations of Royalty being continually deferred to and agreed with. It is easy to tell when she is angry; there is a tightening of the jaw muscles and her voice becomes just slightly shrill. She doesn't rant and rave, shout or scream. She just becomes very Royal indeed.

I once had a brief personal experience of how she can behave towards someone who dares to disagree with her. It happened some years ago in her sitting-room at Buckingham Palace. We were discussing her involvement in Manchester's bid to stage the Olympic Games and I had the temerity to suggest that it was a lost cause and that she was wasting her time and energy in promoting the bid. She icily told me what she thought of my views, and proceeded to give me a verbal roasting, scathingly dismissing my 'defeatist' opinions and apparently taking personally what I had intended as a general comment about the bid.

What I had in fact said was that the press reports I had read revealed that hardly anyone in any other country in the world, Olympic officials and competitors alike, seemed keen on Manchester's charms when compared with other, more glamorous venues such as Atlanta, Tokyo and Sydney. When the vote finally took place, Manchester polled fewer votes than any other city in the running, as also happened when it tried again four years later (although eventually, in 1995, it was given the consolation prize of the

Commonwealth Games in 2002). Manchester had mounted a splendid campaign but was never really in with a serious chance. The Princess simply refused to acknowledge the facts. Determined to be on the winning side, she refused even to consider the possibility of defeat. It was a sentiment to be applauded but one which proved to be unrealistic. Her manner towards me showed that she perhaps considered me as someone who would not normally have been expected to argue, thus revealing a slightly less than tolerant side to her character. It seems she always has to have the last word in any argument.

In fairness, however, I should point out that when I saw her again the day after our little altercation, there was no mention of our previous disagreement. She was perfectly amiable; it was as if nothing had ever happened. In all probability it was so unimportant that she had completely forgotten it. She does not sulk or bear grudges. I was also told (not by her) that I should have felt flattered to have been subjected to such a personal attack as she would not dream of saying such things to a complete stranger. It was in a way a back-handed compliment!

Certainly no one could accuse her of being subject to the unreasonable tantrums, the petty vindictiveness or the unpredictable behaviour that some of the other younger members of the Royal Family have displayed. She has never suffered fools gladly—or even at all—and is known to interrupt (apparently rudely) when her thoughts leap ahead. One thing she can justifiably claim is that she has always been completely consistent. She has never changed her self-imposed rules, even when to do so

3

would have given her much favourable publicity and an adoring press.

The Princess Royal's staff sometimes feel embarrassed by her apparent displays of bad manners, and officials from her organizations such as Save the Children and Riding for the Disabled despair when their Royal Patron does not make the most of what they regard as brilliant and important photo-opportunities. If the Princess Royal's attitude is compared with that of Prince Edward, say, it is clear that she could learn something from her younger brother. If he knows that a reporter or photographer is having transport difficulties in some outlandish spot, he will often offer a seat on the Royal aircraft. The Princess Royal wouldn't dream of doing such a thing—other people's problems in matters like this are no concern of hers. Talk to anyone who has worked with her and the reaction is nearly always the same; they admire her devotion to duty, her willingness to go anywhere on behalf of one of her causes, her single-minded approach to the problems of famine relief, Third World education, child welfare, and so on, and they respect her for being the pragmatic and acceptable face of Royalty at a time when other, younger members of the Royal Family are behaving in a manner which not only brings sadness to the Queen but sullies the reputation of the Monarchy itself. But you rarely hear anyone talk about the Princess Royal with the sort of adoring devotion that, for example, the Princess of Wales can still inspire, in spite of the extraordinary revelations about her marriage. Even the Duchess of York, who has been the subject of more public vilification than any other member of the Royal

Family, is still held in a certain degree of affection by some people in Britain and even more in the United States. And while nobody would compare her workload or standing with that of the Princess Royal—indeed, Lord Charteris, one of the Queen's most respected and revered former Private Secretaries, has described the Duchess as 'vulgar, vulgar, vulgar'—she has nevertheless managed to hold on to a tiny niche in public life. Indeed there are those, including some (but not many) within the Royal Household, who prefer her disposition to that of the Princess Royal. It's not that the Princess is disliked, it's just that no one feels quite at ease with her. As one of the Royal footmen who has worked at Buckingham Palace for many years, remarked, 'She is not the warmest woman I've known.' That is just about the nearest one gets to criticism of HRH.

The Princess loathes having a day off, much to the chagrin of her staff, and says the idea of lying on a beach somewhere soaking up the sun is 'my version of Hell'. She is obsessional about privacy for her children and remains implacably opposed to the suggestion that they should be granted titles. Her son Peter was the first grandchild of any British sovereign to be born a commoner in 500 years. The Queen wanted to give him a title—she still does—but on this matter at least she defers to the wishes of her daughter, and he remains plain Peter Phillips even though he is ninth in line of succession to the throne, above Princess Margaret and his Royal cousins, the Dukes of Gloucester and Kent. Similarly, Mark Phillips declined to accept an earldom when he married Princess Anne (as she then was) and the question has not even arisen with

Tim Laurence.

The Princess's feelings about titles have been well known within the Royal Family for many years, which is partly why it took so long for her to be created Princess Royal. And when this happened, in July 1986, the approach was curiously formal. One might think that the Queen would have simply asked her daughter during one of their fairly frequent meetings whether she would accept the title. But what happened was that Sir William Heseltine, then Her Majesty's Private Secretary, wrote formally to Lieutenant Colonel Peter Gibbs, his opposite number in Princess Anne's office, telling him of the Queen's wishes and asking him to pass on the request. The Princess accepted, and the Queen was told of this in another formal note.

The Princess Royal is a naturally suspicious woman. She does not take easily to strangers, and people with whom she comes into contact on a regular basis find that they have to earn her trust and respect. Once given, however, her friendship is total and she is completely loyal, particularly when someone she has taken into her circle suffers a setback. Two of her Ladies-in-Waiting, the Countess of Lichfield and Caroline Wallace (now Mrs William Nunneley) have been divorced, and when they were going through the throes of that traumatic experience, both found that Princess Anne was there when they needed her. She wasn't a shoulder to cry on; that's not her style. But she did provide comfort and support and included them in a number of engagements when perhaps some others might have excluded them. The fact that she was also friends with both their former husbands, the photographer Patrick Lichfield (who is a distant cousin) and Malcolm Wallace, one of Britain's leading equestrian administrators, made no difference.

The Princess Royal has always prided herself on her parsimony. 'I was brought up by a Scottish nanny to be careful with money and I am by nature someone who hates to see waste,' she once told me when we were talking about how she handled her own funds, and she has never been extravagant in her tastes. Some of the clothes she wears have been in her wardrobe for years. 'A good suit can go on for ever if it's properly made in the first place and has a classic look about it. I expect clothes to last a long time. And I hate buying expensive shoes.' It's not that she dislikes clothes; on the contrary, she quite enjoys dressing up on occasion, but, like her mother, she believes her wardrobe is merely an integral part of the job and certainly not its most important part. She professes not to care if she is criticized for her lack of dress sense, but she is also human enough to be secretly pleased if a picture showing her to her best advantage appears in the papers.

Where her personal features are concerned, photographs almost never do her justice. She has beautiful eyes and a fine complexion, fantastic hair (which she nearly always does herself) and an enviable figure. She is still able to wear the same size 10 clothes she wore twenty years ago and at 5 feet 8 inches tall she can carry off some spectacular outfits when she chooses. She looks truly magnificent in full evening dress with tiara and upswept hair, and wearing some of her outstanding collection of jewels.

The years have been kind to Anne. Taking

regular exercise and still riding, though not competitively, she does not need the services of a personal trainer to keep her stomach taut and flat and there is no hairdresser in constant attention to keep every strand in place or free from intrusive grey. Her hands are those of someone who is used to controlling several tons of horseflesh, with no evidence of a weekly visit from a manicurist.

The Princess of Wales may still be the most photographed woman in the world, and even the Duchess of York gets more coverage than the Princess Royal, but it is the latter who has gained the respect of the media, albeit on occasions rather grudgingly, for her dedication to public life and her example to certain other members of the Royal Family. She has said of herself, 'I never was and never will be a fairy-tale princess.' What she has become is the acceptable face of Royalty at a time when the very institution of Monarchy is threatened by the private lives of some of her closest relatives.

Royal from birth and a direct descendant of Queen Victoria through both her parents, she remains aware that to many members of her family she has always been the odd one out. Knowing from an early age that all the attention was going to be lavished on her brother Charles, she was determined to carve out her own niche in life, and this she has achieved brilliantly, both on the international sporting stage and as an ambassadress for her many charitable causes. She has learnt how to demonstrate a practical understanding of the many complex problems faced by the people who actually work in the field and in doing so she has become much more than just another Royal figurehead. And her courage has never been in doubt, whether on the field in the demanding sport of the Three-Day Event, racing on the Flat or in the rough-and-tumble of the steeplechase, or when she is out and about in the public eye.

I have known the Princess Royal for over twenty-five years, during which time I have seen her develop from a gauche, prickly young girl with a caustic line in humour, who hero-worshipped the sporting giants of the time, into the elegant, much-admired and hard-working woman of today who has survived one broken marriage and made a successful second attempt, and who, if public opinion is anything to go by, would be a popular choice as the next British Sovereign. Over the years I have had many conversations with the Princess Royal about the way she lives her life, the image she has with the press and the public, and her views on being Royal. A few personal observations from these various, mainly unpublished discussions illustrate perhaps some of the reasons why she has been so misunderstood for so many years and how the misconceptions arose. She has been called aggressive, inflexible, frighteningly competitive and totally uncompromising (not meant in a complimentary way). Indeed she has been described as the most competitive member of the Royal Family, mainly because of her sporting achievements and her apparently insatiable appetite for winning.

How does she regard herself? 'I was not in the least competitive in the early days. I had been brought up not to be. You must also remember that girls did not have as many career opportunities

9

then as they do today.'

She regularly tops the league table in Royal duties and is recognized as the hardest-working of all her family. 'There are times when it gets a bit much but generally speaking I don't believe I do any more than anyone else. I do not like sitting around doing nothing, so, if there is a space during the day when I have already got some engagements, I try to fill the time. I see no point in sitting around when perhaps I might be able to make a small contribution by doing something.'

What does she feel about the image she has had for years as a member of the Royal Family who never really fits in? 'I have never been what some people think a Princess should be—wearing a crown and a long dress. And I was always the "tail-end Charlie" and grew up being used to the fact. In my case, having a lot to do with horses has meant getting used to disappointments. You spend years trying to achieve something and just when you think you are there, you are let down. But you have to learn to get on with life which is full of disappointments. The problem is that, as a child, one is rarely prepared for let-downs. You expect everyone to remain the same—and it simply doesn't happen like that. The only advantage of getting older is that you learn a little bit more about understanding other people's problems.'

Did the way the Press seemed to enjoy attacking her for years bother her very much? 'It's too late to do anything about it now but it is pleasant when I see something nice written.'

In March 1974 an armed gunman, Ian Ball, attempted to kidnap Princess Anne in The Mall, shooting and wounding four people, some very seriously (see Chapter 4). How did she feel when this happened? 'Obviously my main concern was for the people who had tried to save me and who had been shot. They were very brave. But my first reaction was anger. I was furious at this man who was having a tug-of-war with me. He ripped my dress, which was a favourite blue one I had made specially to wear away on honeymoon.'

As a former Olympic competitor and now a member of the International Olympic Committee, does she have any views on the way sport has become so professional, and drugs and cheating seem so much a part of everyday events for some athletes? 'I may be naive but my attitude to doping in sport is clear-cut. Cheating is cheating whatever form it takes ... The thing that amazes me about competitors is that most of them know the rules but some choose to take advantage of them in such a way that they don't actually break the letter of the law. Everybody knows what they mean and what they intend. But there's always some silly so-and-so who, because it doesn't actually say you cannot do a certain thing, will always go and do exactly what it doesn't mean.'

What does she think she has gained most from sport? 'Sport has broadened my horizons and competition opened up new experiences. People from all walks of life share a common purpose and common problems.' What has she learnt from being around horses so long? 'Horses are no respecters of rank, ego or wealth and they are definitely character-building.'

The Princess has been accused of being inflexible and using her position to ride roughshod over people who cannot answer back. It has also been said of her that she is uncompromising and will never see the other person's point of view if it does not coincide with her own.

'Completely untrue. I've been a professional fence-sitter all my life. I've had to compromise on many subjects and bite my tongue when I knew in my heart that I was right and someone else was wrong. It's been because of my position that I have had to compromise when I have known that I really wanted to take a very different attitude.'

And what about her relationship with the Queen? Has it been dificult having a mother who is also Head of State?

'It's much more difficult to remember that she is Queen than my mother. After all, I've known her longer as a mother than as a Queen, if you see what I mean. She has been Queen most of my life, but that's not how I think of her—it's the other way round really. As far as my children are concerned, they are not Royal—The Queen just happens to be their grandmother.'

CHAPTER TWO

THE FORMATIVE YEARS

Her Royal Highness Princess Anne of Edinburgh was born ten minutes before noon on Wednesday, 15 August 1950. Two years earlier, when her brother Charles was born, their grandfather, King George VI, had decided that the children of his elder daughter, Princess Elizabeth, were to be known from birth as either Prince or Princess. A

12

special decree published in the *London Gazette* in 1948 stated: 'The children of Princess Elizabeth and the Duke of Edinburgh are to enjoy the style and titular dignity of Prince or Princess before their Christian names.' Had this decree not been issued on the orders of the King, the infant daughter of the then Princess Elizabeth would have been known simply as Lady Anne Mountbatten. She would not have become a Princess until her mother acceded to the throne in 1952. And it was not until her mother became Queen that Anne was permitted to be called The Princess Anne; only the daughters of Sovereigns are allowed the definite article before their names and titles.

Anne was born in Clarence House, at that time her parents' London home, the first child to be born there in well over a hundred years. The birth was straightforward for Princess Elizabeth, so much so that within hours she was calling for State papers so that she could get on with her work. At that time she did not see all the official documents that came to the attention of the King, but for some years, even before she was married, His Majesty had decided that certain papers should be seen by her in preparation for the day when she would become Queen.

Princess Anne was third in line of succession to the throne, behind her mother and brother, and within minutes of the announcement of the birth she received her first public appointment. The Automobile Association made her their one-millionth member, a distinction she was not fully able to appreciate for another eighteen years, until she had passed her driving test and been given her first car.

13

It is difficult to appreciate today just what a Royal birth meant in 1950. Hundreds of people had gathered outside Clarence House waiting for the big event. Some had been there for days, camping out on the pavement. There was a tremendous festive atmosphere and all the comings and goings of various members of the Royal Family were greeted with loud cheers. Finally the crowd's patience was rewarded and a bulletin was issued which announced:

Her Royal Highness the Princess Elizabeth, Duchess of Edinburgh, was safely delivered of a Princess at 11.50 A.M. today. Her Royal Highness and her daughter are doing well. (signed)   WILLIAM GILLIATT
                                            JOHN H. PEEL
                                            VERNON F. HALL
                                            JOHN WEIR

Everyone in the crowd wanted to know how much the baby weighed. The answer? Exactly 6 pounds.

In those days it was not the custom for fathers to be present at the birth of their children and the Duke of Edinburgh (who did not become a Prince until he was given the title by his wife, by then Queen, on 22 February 1957) remained in a room close to the delivery suite, together with his mother-in-law the Queen (now Queen Elizabeth the Queen Mother). For the Duke it was a day of double celebration. He had just learnt that he had been promoted to the rank of Lieutenant Commander in the Royal Navy with an increase in his pay of just over £4 a week.

August is a month when most of the Royal

Family are out of London. The Princess and her husband had remained because it was more convenient for the Royal birth to take place at Clarence House, with the facilities of the best hospitals all nearby in the event of anything going wrong. Similarly, the Queen had delayed her departure for Scotland in order to be close to her daughter. The King, however, had decided that his presence was unnecessary and had gone ahead to Balmoral Castle where he was found shooting on the estate when the news was brought to him by a courtier.

Then the official machinery swung into action. Royal salutes were fired by The King's Troop Royal Horse Artillery in Hyde Park and answered from the Tower of London by the guns of the Honourable Artillery Company. Many people had to be informed of the birth, including the Prime Minister and the Lord Mayor of London. No minister of the Crown had been needed to witness it, as had been the custom until Prince Charles was born, when his grandfather, King George VI, decided that nobody was likely to claim that another baby had been substituted for the Royal infant, as had happened in centuries past.

The Governors-General of the Dominions and all foreign ambassadors in London were informed, and in keeping with an ancient tradition, letters were despatched to Edinburgh to tell the Lord Provost, the Lord President of the Court of Session, the Lord Advocate and the Lord Justice Clerk. The Duke of Edinburgh undertook to tell the family and telephoned his mother at her apartments in Kensington Palace. He was unable to speak directly to Queen Mary, the Queen Mother,

15

who was staying at Sandringham, as she always refused to talk on the telephone, so a Lady-in-Waiting carried the message to her that she had a second great-grandchild.

Two weeks later the full names of the child were announced. She was to be called Anne Elizabeth Alice Louise, all long-time family favourites. The choice of Anne was something of a surprise because when Princess Margaret was born in 1930, and her mother wanted to name her Ann, as she thought Ann of York 'had a nice ring to it', she was persuaded not to do so because her father-in-law, King George V, did not care for the name. Elizabeth was self-explanatory as a second name, while Alice was chosen to honour the Duke of Edinburgh's mother who was known as Princess Andrew, with only her closest relatives using her given name. Louise was another favourite, having been the Christian name of King Edward VII's eldest daughter, and coincidentally a former Princess Royal, who later became Duchess of Fife. Louise was also chosen as a tribute to Earl Mountbatten of Burma, the Duke of Edinburgh's uncle, whose name was Louis.

Two months after she was born the Princess was christened in the Music Room at Buckingham Palace, used for Royal christenings since the chapel at the Palace had been destroyed by enemy bombs during the Second World War. On 21 October 1950 five sponsors (the Royal Family does not have godparents) gathered for the ceremony. They had been chosen with great care after discussion with the King and Queen and other members of the family. The Queen herself was the first sponsor, a break with tradition as previously Sovereigns and their consorts did not act in this capacity. However, King George VI had suggested himself as a sponsor for his grandson, Prince Charles, two years earlier, causing a certain amount of consternation among some of his older courtiers at the time. Princess Andrew of Greece was also a sponsor but did not attend the ceremony as she was abroad; Princess Alice of Athlone, a granddaughter of Queen Victoria, acted as her proxy. Princess Margarita of Hohenlohe-Langenburg, the Duke of Edinburgh's elder sister, Earl Mountbatten and the Hon. Andrew Elphinstone, Princess Elizabeth's first cousin, were the others.

The Archbishop of York, Dr Garbett, performed the ceremony as the Archbishop of Canterbury, who would have normally been in charge of such an event, was in Australia. No outsiders were present, only the immediate family, and the verdict on the behaviour of the principal guest was that she performed impeccably.

The infant was handed over to the care of a Scottish nanny, Helen Lightbody, and her assistant, Mabel Anderson. They were both experienced in bringing up Royal children, Miss Anderson having looked after Prince William and Prince Richard of Gloucester in their early years.

Anne, like her brother Charles, was brought up in typical upper-class fashion. Her parents were absent much of the time; the Duke of Edinburgh, as a serving officer in the Royal Navy, was with his ship, and Princess Elizabeth was taking on many of the public duties her father would have carried out had it not been for his ill-health.

Within eighteen months of Anne's birth the entire domestic life of the Edinburghs changed for ever. On 6 February 1952 King George VI died in his sleep at Sandringham and his daughter became Queen Elizabeth II. She was twenty-five when she became the forty-second Sovereign of England since William the Conqueror, yet only its sixth Queen Regnant. For the Duke of Edinburgh it was a traumatic time as he now had to learn to walk slightly behind his wife whenever they were seen in public and for the rest of his life his own career and ambitions would be secondary to the demands and requirements of the Crown.

The family moved across the road to Buckingham Palace, and Grannie, the Queen Mother, moved into Clarence House. Anne, of course, was completely unaware of any alteration in her circumstances, or the fact that she was now second in the line of succession. It was the closest she would ever get and as, in later years, two more brothers were born and eventually both Charles and Andrew had children of their own, she moved farther and farther down the order.

For the time being Anne had simply changed one nursery for another and even her relationship with her parents remained the same. She and Charles saw their mother and father for half an hour in the morning, then again in the late afternoon before they were bathed and packed off to bed. The long absences enforced by the Queen's overseas tours following her Coronation in 1953 meant that Anne grew accustomed to not seeing her parents for weeks, sometimes months on end. Years later she explained how her own children had become used to the same system: 'They have grown up knowing I have to be away for long periods and they have got used to it. They don't see anything out of the ordinary in my being away from home.'

Anne and her brother Charles began their education in the Buckingham Palace schoolroom on the second floor, where today the Princess has her suite of offices. Miss Catherine Peebles was engaged as governess to Charles with whom she quickly became so besotted that when Anne was sent along for lessons she was practically ignored. Miss Peebles was totally possessive about Charles: he could do no wrong in her eyes and she hated leaving him for a moment, even when he was spending time with his mother. It was not a healthy relationship and Charles became equally dependent on her. When it was decided to send him away to preparatory school at the age of seven, Miss Peebles was distraught. She wept for days and when two five-year-old girls, Susan (Sukie) Babington-Smith and Caroline Hamilton, both granddaughters of senior courtiers, were brought into the Palace to share Anne's lessons, there was never any great enthusiasm from any of those involved.

Several years later, after Anne had herself left for Benenden boarding school, Miss Peebles died in her room at Buckingham Palace. There was a big question mark over her death, mainly because her body remained undiscovered for several days, and when Charles was given the news he was inconsolable. Anne said later that the only emotion she felt 'was a sense of guilt because I could not grieve as sincerely as my brother'.

The Palace schoolroom operated for seven years, until Anne was twelve, then the three girls who had spent nearly all their waking hours together were split up. Sukie Babington-Smith

19

(now Mrs John Hemming) says it was deliberate: 'I'm quite sure it was laid down by the Queen and her advisers that we should be split up, and I'm equally sure it was the right thing to do, even though at the time it seemed rather brutal. We never wrote to each other after leaving the Palace, we didn't even have a farewell party; there was no contact.' Nor was there subsequently. The Princess made no attempt to contact her earliest schoolfriends and when I put it to her that it was unusual that such a close relationship should have ended so abruptly, she replied, 'They know where I am, they can telephone at any time.' That is probably quite true. They could have got in touch if they had wanted to but it is also understandable that they did not. In the same way that Anne's fellow pupils at Benenden were careful not to be seen to try to curry favour with their Royal schoolmate, it would be difficult for Sukie and Caroline to ring the Palace and ask for the Princess Royal without appearing to be social climbers. That is not the way she herself would see it—though she is able to spot a phoney at a hundred paces—but it is easy to see why they should hesitate.

Princess Anne started her first term at Benenden on 20 September 1963. At that time the annual fees were £525. All forty staff and 300 pupils were lined up in front of the school to greet their Royal colleague but they had to wait for half an hour as Anne had been sick in the car. So the cool, exterior public face which even then she showed to outsiders, concealed the normal first-day nerves experienced by any girl of her age.

Entrance to the school was usually by written examination, an ordeal spared the Princess because, as the headmistress, the late Miss Elizabeth Clarke, explained, 'I had been invited to Windsor Castle to meet the Queen and Prince Philip for a general chat. Some days later I received a personal telephone call from Her Majesty telling me it had been decided to send Princess Anne to Benenden, if she was acceptable. I then spoke to the Princess's tutors at Buckingham Palace and they satisfied me that she was up to our academic standards so I decided to take her without the examination requirement.' Miss Clarke denied that there was any question of favouritism, saying, 'It was important that she could keep up. Otherwise it would not have been fair to the school or to her.' As it happened, Anne had few difficulties apart from mathematics, a subject in which she had little interest, and as Benenden at that time did not have a particularly outstanding academic record anyway she fitted in as an average pupil, which is what she—and the Queen—wanted. As the daughter of the Sovereign, however, she was obviously not just like all the others. She was the only girl with a personal police officer, David Coleman, in attendance, and when her mother came to visit, as she did frequently in the early years, police were stationed at every crossroads along the route, making sure all the lights were green. The Queen took a close interest in her daughter's education and frequently rang the headmistress to check on her progress. Miss Clarke recalled, 'Once you became used to the fact that it really was the Queen on the telephone, the chats became very relaxed and informal.'

Anne made many acquaintances at school but few lasting friendships. One of her Ladies-in-

Waiting, Victoria Legge-Bourke, was also at Benenden, but she was a year ahead of the Princess so had little to do with her. In fact she can barely remember talking to her in their schooldays, so it was not a case of old schoolfriends meeting up when she was invited to become a member of the Princess's Household (see Chapter 12).

At the end of her five years at Benenden the Princess emerged with two A-level passes in history and geography. Although this result was not brilliant, at that time it was enough to have gained a place at one of the lesser universities. Princess Anne decided not to apply, however, and today she still thinks she was right. 'You must remember that girls did not have as many career opportunities in those days, and in my case there were added difficulties obviously, so I think I was right in deciding not to apply for university at the time.'

She also left Benenden with one other distinction. She was the only girl in the school who always had something left over from her £2 a term pocket money, and indeed still describes herself as being 'mean with money' as the result of her upbringing by a canny Scottish nanny.

Thus, at eighteen, Anne ended her formal education and began a career of public duties almost immediately. From then until the present day, she would assume a role in the life of the nation that would see her travel the world on behalf of her many charities. She is probably most closely identified with Save the Children, but this is only one of the 300 charities she works for. She became her mother's most valued support at home and abroad and by the diligence of her efforts would restore much of the prestige of a Monarchy damaged by the questionable behaviour of her siblings and their spouses.

CHAPTER THREE

ANNE AND MARK

When Princess Anne married Mark Phillips in a fairytale ceremony in Westminster Abbey, it seemed the perfect culmination of a Royal love story. The honeymoon was spent on the Royal Yacht *Britannia*, courtesy of the Queen, and over a thousand wedding presents worth well over £2 million were waiting to be enjoyed when the couple returned home.

Mark was set for a promising career in one of the Army's most fashionable regiments. There were a couple of minor irritations that he would have to overcome, such as the fact that while his pay was just over £90 a week, Anne's weekly income from the Civil List was around £1200, plus an undisclosed sum from a Trust Fund set up for her by the Queen. It was not the ideal way to start married life, knowing that you could never match the style in which your wife had been brought up. It must have been frustrating to Mark to realize that the cars, servants, furniture and their future homes would all come from the purse of the woman he had married. The couple never had a joint bank account. They maintained separate accounts, with Anne's office paying all the household expenses and Mark, despite all his good intentions, contributing precisely nothing to the upkeep of their home.

At first the Army provided the Phillipses with married quarters at Sandhurst, at a highly subsidized rent. Although Mark had only just been promoted to Captain, the house they were allocated would normally have been reserved for an officer of the rank of at least Lieutenant Colonel. Obviously there was no question of letting the Queen's only daughter live in a 'semi' like any ordinary Army wife, so Oak Grove House, an elegant five-bedroomed detached property standing in its own grounds in a secluded part of the Sandhurst College estate, was made available. The rent was £400 a year (or just under £8 a week) including electricity, heating and rates, and to make sure it was suitable for the couple, some £25,000 was spent on refurbishing. A public right-of-way which ran close to the property was diverted and a special security system was installed. Naturally this aroused enormous 'indignation' in the tabloid press but in fact the authorities responsible (not the Army but the Department of the Environment) had spent only £5,000 of public money—the remaining £20,000 had come from the pocket of Princess Anne herself and had been released to her on the authority of Lord Porchester (now the Earl of Carnarvon), the senior administrator of her Trust Fund.

Normally when an officer (or indeed a soldier of any rank) moves into married quarters, all his furniture is provided by the Army. In the case of the newly-wed Phillipses this was not necessary. Practically everything they needed had been given as wedding presents—dining-room suite, drawing-room furniture, carpets from Iran and even a 200-

year-old grandfather clock from the City of Westminster. The wallpaper they used to decorate the house was guaranteed to be exclusive; it came from a private stock of patterns held at Buckingham Palace which could not be bought by ordinary members of the public. Even their coat-hangers had a Royal connection as they had been given eight dozen by Princess Margaretha of Sweden.

As the couple settled down to married life, the rumours about Princess Anne's former love life fizzled out. Her name had been linked with practically every eligible European prince and princeling and many grandees' sons as the British and Continental press sought to marry her off. In truth she had never seriously considered marrying any of them. She was determined that if and when she married it would be to someone she cared for and whose pedigree would be of little importance. Prince (later King) Carl Gustav of Sweden was thought to be a leading contender for a while. But at thirty-three he was thought to be slightly too old—not a consideration that dissuaded Prince Charles when he married in 1981—and the Princess let it be known that she was not too impressed by his lack of humour and stiff Court manners. Other would-be husbands who were thought to be in the running included her second cousin, Patrick, Earl of Lichfield, one of the world's most famous photographers, who eventually married—and was divorced by—Leonora, sister of the Duke of Westminster, who is now a Lady-in-Waiting to the Princess Royal.

Among the other aristocrats who escorted the Princess and so immediately became candidates in the marriage stakes were Earl Alexander of Tunis, son of one of Britain's greatest heroes of the Second World War, and another earl, this time of Suffolk and Berkshire, whose claims were dismissed mainly because he was divorced—in the early seventies, no one involved in a divorce case, even if an 'innocent' party, was admitted to Court or allowed to work in the Royal Household.

Perhaps the two most serious contenders were Richard Meade and Sandy Harper. Meade, arguably the most successful Three-Day Eventer Britain has ever produced, was already a legend among his contemporaries, with double Olympic Gold Medals to his credit. He and Princess Anne were attracted to each other and saw a great deal of one another for quite some time before Mark Phillips came on the scene. The Princess was besotted and hero-worshipped Meade for a while. Tall, fair-haired, with perfect manners, he appeared to many people to be the ideal partner for her. Unfortunately for him he was twelve years older and also quite independent. Insiders at Buckingham Palace claimed that the Duke of Edinburgh didn't get on with him, and as far as Anne is concerned, her father can do no wrong. Anyway, Meade disappeared from the scene and some years later made a very happy marriage.

Sandy Harper was 'something in the City' and spent most of his spare time playing polo. He too was nearly twelve years older than the Princess but was considered to be one of the most eligible bachelors in London and a number of senior courtiers felt he was the one Anne would go for. Only the two of them know the truth behind their break-up, whether he was dropped by her or if it was his decision to call it a day. Whatever the reason, he married a well-known fashion model, Peta Secombe, whom he later lost to another polo player, an Argentinian.

A name which meant very little to the public in those days but which has come to be as well known as almost any in the land today, is that of Andrew Parker Bowles. As a young cavalry officer he was a frequent escort to the Princess in her late teens, and as someone who knew the form at Buckingham Palace he might have been thought of as suitable husband material. But the one major drawback, and one which he would have felt it impossible to overcome, was that he is a Roman Catholic. In those days the idea of a Catholic joining the Royal Family was unthinkable—Princess Michael of Kent had yet to be admitted—particularly as at that time Princess Anne was still reasonably close to the Throne in the line of succession.

The list of possible husbands grew longer every day. In fact, Anne only had to be seen in the company of almost any eligible young man for him to be mentioned as a possible future husband. It didn't do the reputations of her escorts any harm; most of whom were delighted to have their names linked with the Princess. At parties held in London and at country houses, quite a number of young men liked to boast quietly of their close friendship with Her Royal Highness. Strangely enough, though, there was never even a whisper of any nocturnal goings-on. If anything like that had occurred it could not have remained a secret; someone would have been bound to talk. But Princess Anne's reputation as something of a flirt—she has always liked men, preferring their

27

company to that of women and she does possess an enormous amount of sex appeal, and knows it!—went no further. And even today, when newspapers offer tremendous sums of money for kiss-and-tell stories involving any member of the Royal Family, no one has ever come forward claiming to have slept with her. As one of her early Australian would-be suitors rather picturesquely put it, 'None of us got past the prickles to taste the goodies.'

The soldiers in Princess Anne's regiments dote on her and are all very much aware of her attractions. It's common knowledge in the various messes she visits that men of every rank, not only officers, all 'fancy her like mad'. A young corporal in the 14/20th Hussars, the first regiment to invite her to become their Colonel-in-Chief, and the one which gave her the personal number plate 1420H as a twenty-first birthday present, said after she had spent a few days with them in Germany, 'She's one of the few women I've seen who looks sexy in tank overalls.' Princess Anne is lucky enough to have the body of a finely tuned athlete, without the muscles, which has barely changed since she was eighteen, and on which riding clothes look most attractive.

Another, less obviously attractive facet of her character, but one which makes her appealing to men, is her sense of humour. 'She's very funny,' says one of her oldest friends. 'I know that sometimes she looks po-faced but underneath she is witty, very intelligent, with a wicked line in humour.' Those in the know say her humour tends to be on the cruel and sarcastic side, but only with those she knows well. Her manners are impeccable with strangers and one way to gauge your personal standing with her is if she makes you the butt of one of her jokes. Only real 'insiders' feel the full force of her acid wit.

When Anne first started to show an interest in Mark Phillips, it came as something of a surprise to many of the people in the horsey world who knew them both. Anne has a mercurial temperament; some days she is on a high, on others she can be very low-spirited. Mark, however, was, and is, a much quieter and less temperamental person. He was able to ride the storms of her occasional bad temper, often by simply laughing it off, and in doing so he was usually able to laugh her out of it as well.

If Anne had plenty of admirers when they met, Mark also had his fair share of fans among their set. Lucinda Prior-Palmer (now Green), Jane Bullen (now Holderness-Roddam and a Lady-in-Waiting to the Princess Royal) and one or two others all freely admitted that they 'adored Mark', but he had eyes only for Anne practically from the moment they first met. They quickly became an item at Badminton, Burghley and all the other venues throughout the country where Three-Day Events were held, and the rest of the girls realized that one of the favourite 'jockeys' had been captured.

When Princess Anne married Captain Mark Phillips in 1973 there was no question of political or monarchical expediency, which for centuries had been a prime consideration in the marriages of British Princesses. Anne's choice of husband was hers alone and the fact that he was untitled and not even the heir to a vast fortune or great estates did not come into it.

In fact, although Mark had a typical middle-class

background in many ways, there were also traces of a grander strain among his ancestors. His maternal grandfather, Brigadier John Tiarks, was a regular at Court and became a valued and trusted Aide to King George VI. Mark's own father, Major Peter Phillips, had served honourably in the Army as a regular officer, having joined the King's Dragoon Guards straight from school and been awarded the Military Cross during the Second World War. The KDGs (or Queen's Dragoon Guards as they are now known) was the family regiment, with Mark's father, maternal grandfather (who commanded the regiment from 1939), uncle and godfather all having served in it at some time.

When he left the Army, Major Peter Phillips had intended to join the family's mining engineering business, but the postwar Labour Government's nationalization strategies put an end to those plans. Instead he took a course at agricultural college (as his son would many years later) and began farming in Gloucestershire, where he bought 400 acres. However, his inexperience, coupled with the fact that he was short of money, meant that his farming career ended abruptly after a nine-year struggle. He later admitted his business failings, saying, 'I was under-capitalized and made some mistakes which were difficult to rectify and when they put a motorway through the best part of my farm that was that.' He then joined the firm of Walls, of ice-cream and sausages fame, in 1957, as an area manager and rose to become a director of the company before he retired.

Mark's late mother, Anne, was a member of the old-established Tiarks banking family, and when the engagement was announced his grandmother

Tiarks said, 'It's a feather in the family's cap to have a Royal among us.' Anne Phillips, who preferred to remain in the background throughout all the publicity surrounding her son's involvement with Princess Anne, said that his entry into the Royal Family would not change the Phillipses' way of life, which was a quiet country existence.

Mark was born on 22 September 1948 at Tetbury in Gloucestershire, but by the time he met the Princess Royal, the family had moved to the village of Great Somerford in Wiltshire, just a few miles from his eventual home at Gatcombe Park. He has one sister, Sarah, born in 1951, who is now Mrs Frank Staples.

His education was fairly conventional. After starting at Wells Court junior school near his home at the age of five, he was sent away to board at Stouts Hill preparatory school when he was eight and then, after passing his Common Entrance examination, he went to Marlborough College, one of England's leading public schools. Slightly below average scholastically at first, he excelled in sports, playing rugby and cricket for the school. But it was as a horseman that he really shone. He was one of those who literally grew up in the saddle. His mother had been a brilliant horsewoman herself, and was a former Master of the local hunt at Great Somerford, so it was natural that Mark would ride from an early age. Indeed he could ride before he could walk and his parents gave him his first pony when he was just eighteen months old.

At school Mark excelled at athletics, competing in the high, long and triple jumps, and he was a very useful three-quarter, winning a place in the Colts XV but not quite making it to the 1st team.

He was elected Captain of Athletics and made a prefect and, in the fifth form at Marlborough, after working very hard, gained eight O-levels. In his final year he obtained two A-levels (like Princess Anne, in history and geography), which should have been sufficient for him to obtain direct entry to Sandhurst as an officer cadet.

Mark was keenly disappointed when the Regular Commission Board failed him in 1966, as it had always been assumed by the family that he would naturally follow his father into his old regiment. Determined to succeed, however, he enlisted in April 1967 as a private soldier (or rifleman) in the Royal Green Jackets. There he was quickly singled out as potential officer material and within four months was admitted to Sandhurst as a cadet. It was while he was still at the College that he was selected as a member of the British Team for the 1968 Olympic Games, and that was when he first met his future wife.

Upon graduation, in July 1969, he was commissioned as a 2nd Lieutenant in 1st The Queen's Dragoon Guards, which like all cavalry regiments had been converted to tanks. It must have been a source of great personal satisfaction to Mark that when the results of the final examinations at Sandhurst were published, he came second out of an entry of 300—not bad for someone who had originally been rejected as unsuitable. He was posted to the regiment's headquarters at Detmold in what was then West Germany, where be became a troop leader. His immediate superior officer was Captain Eric Grounds, who would be Mark's best man at the Royal Wedding in 1973.

Horses still played a major part in the lives of many of the officers and Mark found a perfect niche for himself. There was plenty of time for play and, as an already accomplished horseman in national competitions, he was given ample opportunities to pursue his riding ambitions. The Army has always regarded sport as an important and integral part of training and anyone who shows talent is encouraged to go all the way, as sporting success is seen as an indirect aid to recruiting. So when Mark began to win competitions in Three-Day Events, his commanding officer allowed him all the time he needed to train and every assistance was given to the young officer to take him right to the top.

His international equestrian success began when he became a member of the British team at the 1968 Mexico Olympic Games, and he was included in the official team at the 1970 World Championships and the European Championships in 1971, which is when he also won the first of his four Badminton titles (1971, '72, '74, '81). He again represented Britain at the Munich Olympics in 1972, but in 1976, at the Montreal Games, in spite of being chosen for the squad, he was relegated to the position of reserve and had to sit and watch his wife who had made the team.

Mark was a competent and popular officer and his climb to the top of his profession might have continued unimpeded had he not married into the Royal Family. Soon after the wedding it was revealed that the regiment was shortly to leave for a tour in Northern Ireland and newspapers began speculating about whether Mark would go too. As it happened, he had already been posted to

Sandhurst as an instructor, so the problem was avoided, but the incident did raise the question of how a career officer who had become a member of the Royal Family could continue without accompanying his men to the trouble spots of the world. Northern Ireland would have been impossible at that time as Mark would have been seen as not only a legitimate target but also a highly sought-after one. His security would have posed tremendous problems for his superiors and might also have endangered other men. Nevertheless, Mark knew that unless he was to be allowed to go wherever the regiment went, he would never rise to a position where he might be considered as a future commanding officer. So, in effect, his marriage meant the end of his military career. He realized early on that he would have to get out and earn a living in civilian life, and the only way he would be able to do that was by using his talent with horses.

When Mark did eventually leave the Army his business career took off almost immediately. He was in constant demand all over the world, holding master-classes in advanced riding for which students paid up to £300 a day; and as his success grew on the competition field, sponsors lined up to throw money at him. Land Rover were first, with a £20,000-a-year contract for three years, and others followed close behind.

Mark went to the Royal Agricultural College at Cirencester, taking a course in farming which he later put into practice running the 1200-acre estate at Gatcombe Park, which the Queen bought for Princess Anne in 1976. Unfortunately the land at Gatcombe has never been particularly fertile so the estate has never made a profit, and because Mark

34

was abroad so often and for such long periods, the day-to-day organization of the farm was left to a management company based in Cambridge. Still, when he was home, he took an active role in the farm, and at harvest-time Anne and her brothers Andrew and Edward would all lend a hand in the fields.

Throughout their entire married life—which lasted sixteen years until the separation—Mark struggled to come to terms with his wife's position and the fact that she had much more money than himself. It was a situation which Prince Philip, Angus Ogilvy and Lord Snowdon had all had to face, but nobody offered Mark any advice on how to cope. And it seemed that no matter how hard he worked, or how successful he was in business, the only place where he was superior to his wife was in the saddle. That, of course, had been the reason why she respected him so much in the first place. He was one of the very few people she knew she would never be able to beat on a horse.

In addition he never found his public role an easy one. The Princess knew of his problems and sympathized, saying, 'You have to have something to call your own.' The idea of opting out of public life was never an option for her, but she realized how difficult it was for a man who was essentially a private person to be suddenly catapulted into a world where every aspect of his life—not just his sporting achievements—was subject to the closest scrutiny. Mark hated every minute of it. He would gladly have existed without any sort of Press attention, apart from the publicity he needed and accepted as an international competitor. I spoke to him many times about his career as a rider and as an organizer of the Gatcombe Horse Trials and he freely admitted to me that every public appearance was 'pure torture'—something that had to be endured but never enjoyed.

Another of the difficulties the couple encountered was that Mark has never been particularly decisive: he finds it easier to go along with other people's decisions. The Princess Royal, on the other hand, makes all her own decisions, most of them instantaneously. Within two years of their marriage she had become the dominant partner, and Mark just drifted with the tide. He didn't always like it; he simply did not do anything about it. He did not seem to realize that the Princess needed, and still needs, a man who will stand up to her, and this is where Tim Laurence scores heavily over Mark.

Since the divorce, without having to live his life constantly on the lookout for the media, Mark has become a much more relaxed personality. His father, Major Peter Phillips, with whom the Princess Royal still enjoys a warm relationship, now lives with Mark on the Gatcombe Park estate and relies greatly on his son. They were both devastated when Mark's mother, Anne Phillips, died in 1988, and the Princess was equally distressed. In spite of her own marriage difficulties, she had always had a warm regard for her mother-in-law, and she was one of a small group of family mourners who attended the funeral service in Great Somerford, where she still visits the grave in the village churchyard.

Being away from the spotlight that accompanies Royalty wherever it goes means that Mark can live his life fairly privately, though not entirely so. Once you have been associated with the Royal Family you are never completely free from publicity, and for the rest of his life Mark will always be known as the man who was once married to the Queen's daughter. If he has any regrets he keeps them to himself, and if there is one thing that the Princess Royal can be absolutely certain of, it is that Mark will never ever be tempted to 'tell all'.

In a happy postscript to the Anne and Mark story, he remarried on 1 February 1997 in Hawaii. His bride, the American heiress Sandy Pflueger, was also a member of the United States international equestrian team, of which Mark is the coach. In sharp contrast to his first wedding, this one took place on a tropical beach with just a hundred family and friends present. Mark and Sandy spend part of their time in the United States, with their main base remaining at Mark's Aston Farm on the Gatcombe estate.

CHAPTER FOUR

GUNFIRE ON THE MALL

On Wednesday, 20 March 1974, the Queen could easily have lost her only daughter. On that day an armed gunman tried to kidnap Princess Anne in The Mall, and in the attempt shot and wounded four people. It was only with the greatest of luck, her own presence of mind, and the bravery of those around her that Princess Anne's life was saved and she emerged unharmed.

The Princess and her husband, Mark Phillips,

had been married a little over four months, and they had moved into their first home, Oak Grove House at the Royal Military College, Sandhurst, just five weeks before the incident that was to change Royal security for ever took place. Both Anne and Mark were keenly interested in the charity Riding for the Disabled and they had agreed to attend a special showing of a film, *Riding for Freedom*, which told the story of the organization. It was to be screened in a studio at Sudbury House, Newgate Street, near Ludgate Circus in the heart of the City of London.

The evening passed without incident, and the Royal limousine, an ancient Austin Princess (registration number NGN 1), driven by fifty-five-year-old Alex Callendar, one of the Queen's most experienced and trusted chauffeurs, with more than twenty years in Royal service, left for the fifteen-minute drive back to Buckingham Palace where the couple were to pick up their own car to return to Sandhurst. Sitting alongside Mr Callendar was Inspector James Beaton, the Princess's police bodyguard, while the 'jump' seat was occupied by Rowena Brassey, the Lady-in-Waiting.

The time was just after 7.30 p.m.; the City streets were deserted and traffic was light. The weather was dry and cold. The route the car would take had been agreed earlier by the travel office in the Royal Mews: Newgate Street, Fleet Street, The Strand, Trafalgar Square, through Admiralty Arch and down The Mall to the Palace, where they were due to arrive at 7.50 p.m.

In those days Royal cars frequently travelled alone, without the protection of a police back-up

38

vehicle or outriders to clear the road in front. After that night they would never travel unaccompanied again.

As the Austin Princess moved away from Sudbury House, no one took the slightest notice of a white Ford Escort that slid into place just behind them—there was no reason why they should. It followed the Royal car through Fleet Street, kept close behind in The Strand and was on their tail as they crossed Trafalgar Square and headed down The Mall.

At the wheel of the Escort was an armed madman, about to carry out one of the most audacious crimes of the century. It would be the climax of three years' planning and preparation which would, if all went according to plan, bring him £3 million. The twenty-six-year-old, though subsequently proved to be mentally unstable, had used all the cunning and meticulous attention to detail of a master criminal. A web of false addresses and identities had been established; all the labels from his clothes had been destroyed, as had his passport in his real name of Ian Ball. His driving licence was false, issued in the name of John Williams—one of three aliases he used to try to obliterate his past, and the car he was driving had been hired, also using his false name.

Ball was a small-time crook who had been arrested three times for receiving stolen property and obtaining goods by deception. He could only be identified by the fingerprints on his police record, and after that night he would secure his own dubious place in history and see his name on the front pages of every newspaper in the world.

Ball lived in a fantasy world of his own. He had

no friends, and after leaving the parental home to live alone in cheap lodgings, his sole passion was the flying lessons he paid for himself. He desperately wanted to make a financial killing and formed his plan to kidnap Princess Anne with chilling precision. He had followed her unobserved for months, so that he could recognize her Ladies-in-Waiting and personal police officers. Knowing her bodyguard would be armed, he went to great lengths to get a gun for himself. Not wanting to run the risk of trying to buy one in Britain he travelled to Spain where he easily obtained a firearms permit and then bought four weapons in a shop in the Plaza de España in Madrid. Taking no chances, he bought two Astra revolvers, a five-round .38 and an eleven-round .22. In the comparatively terrorist-free atmosphere of 1974 (even though the IRA were active) it was relatively simple to smuggle the weapons into England.

Then it was time for the second phase of his preparations. Much publicity had been given to the fact that the Princess and her husband were taking over a new house at Sandhurst, and the address was common knowledge. So Ball scouted the area looking for a suitable place he could rent nearby where he could take the Princess once he had captured her. He found the ideal spot: a smart four-bedroomed detached property, 17 Silverdale, a quiet, tree-lined cul-de-sac in Fleet, Hampshire, a few minutes' drive from Oak Grove House. It was known locally as 'Brigadiers' Row' because of the number of senior army officers living there. Ball found it remarkably easy to rent the house in yet another of his aliases, Jason Van der Sluis, a name he had acquired by the simple expedient of stealing a letter addressed to the real Mr Van der Sluis from the members' pigeon-holes at a London club. As Ball also found out from this letter that the member had an account at Barclays Bank in Covent Garden, he was able to give this information to the estate agents when they asked for references. He provided further false references for himself by using accommodation addresses.

Paying a cash deposit and £27 as a month's rent in advance, Ball was given the tenancy of the house and moved in shortly before the attempted kidnap. The curtains were kept tightly closed day and night and Ball spent the time listening to records of classical music and refining his plans. He used the weeks before 20 March to stock the house with everything he thought he would need to keep Princess Anne reasonably happy during her captivity. He bought bedding, night-clothes, new towels, a toothbrush and a supply of food, in case the negotiations went on for some time. He even fitted new locks on the bathroom and lavatory doors, which could be opened from the outside, so that the Princess would not be able to lock herself in.

It was obvious that his original intention had been to attack her somewhere near her home and not in central London. Even if he had managed to get her away in The Mall, the journey to Surrey would have been almost impossible without attracting a posse of police cars. It would have been much easier to spirit her a few miles through country lanes if his initial plan had worked.

Once the house was ready to receive its unwilling guest, Ball proceeded with the final preparations. In order to write the ransom note and another letter to a firm of solicitors he wanted to act as middlemen, he hired a typewriter from a shop in Camberley. The shop assistant who served him thought it strange that Ball said he wanted the typewriter for only a single day, and for the sake of £1.50—the cost of the one day's hire—the whole plan might have been destroyed if only these suspicions had been taken further.

Less than eight hours before the kidnap attempt Ball had another lucky escape when a detective chief inspector noticed his hired car parked near the rear entrance to Sandhurst. He was asked to produce his driving licence, which he did (in the false name) and his car was searched, but nothing was found and he was allowed to leave. The reason he was questioned had nothing to do with the security of the Princess, but because there had been a spate of robberies in the area. A non-commissioned officer based at Sandhurst had also noticed the car, even noting the registration number, SVL 282 L, on no fewer than eleven occasions over a three-day period. It was probably Ball's lucky escape with the police in Surrey that prompted him into taking the action in London that was to lead to near tragedy.

At around 7.40 p.m. on that fateful Wednesday, Alex Callendar turned the Royal car into The Mall. Princess Anne and Mark Phillips were sitting together in the back with Rowena Brassey (now Mrs Andrew Feilden) just in front of them on the fold-up seat behind the partition that divided them from the chauffeur and Inspector James Beaton. Beaton had been appointed to guard the Princess on her wedding day, 14 November 1973. At that time he was a sergeant and had been promoted shortly after.

They were less than four hundred yards from Buckingham Palace, just after the Marlborough Road turn-off at St James's Palace, when Ball struck. He accelerated sharply and overtook the Princess's car, then pulled his Ford Escort in front of the limousine and forced it to brake fiercely to avoid a collision. At this point the chauffeur and Inspector Beaton acted in a way that seemed inexplicable in retrospect, but was perfectly understandable at the time. They stopped the car and Beaton got out to see what was wrong. Today it would be seen as a classic case of doing the wrong thing at the wrong time. Security training these days instructs drivers—and policemen—that in such an instance all the doors should be locked, windows shut, and the car—which was much more powerful than the Escort—should have reversed at speed and then driven straight into the Palace forecourt. They could even have driven right at the Escort and pushed it out of the way if necessary.

But, as Jim Beaton now explains, the whole atmosphere was different then; international terrorism had not reared its head and the thought of anyone attempting to harm a member of the Royal Family was laughable. 'When the Escort pulled up in front of us and the driver leapt out, my first thought was that perhaps Alex Callendar had cut him up somewhere along the route and he was going to tell him what he thought of him. Even that was unusual then; road rage hadn't been heard of either. So I got out of the car to explain who we were and to try and settle things quietly. I didn't want him seeing the Princess and starting a fuss. To show you just how different things were in those days, I was going to leave the Princess and Mark at the Palace so they could drive back to Sandhurst on their own and I was going to go to my own home. Policemen didn't travel everywhere with the Royals; there was no need. And you must remember that I was the Princess's only police officer. There was no large team like there is today; it was me on my own.'

Ball leaped out of his car and ran towards the Royal car shooting as he ran. The first shot smashed one of the rear windows. Inspector Beaton's first thought was to protect the Princess so he ran round to her side of the car where Ball was trying to open the door. Ball's second shot hit Jim Beaton in the chest, causing his right lung to collapse. Although Beaton still managed to fire off one shot, which missed, owing to his injury, he was unable to fire again because his gun jammed. Jim Beaton continues his story, 'When I first heard the crack of the gun I knew something serious was happening, but I didn't feel a thing when he shot me. I just felt a bit hazy and I couldn't raise my arm so I used both hands to shoot back. The amazing thing was that I actually had the gun with me. The weapon was allocated to Princess Anne (as she then was) and just before we left the Palace for the City I went to my room to tidy up a bit. There was a bed alongside the door and I threw the gun on to it, intending to leave it there until we came back. Then I thought that perhaps somebody would come in to make up the bed and if they saw the gun there might be questions asked. So I tucked it into my waistband. Otherwise I wouldn't even have bothered with it.'

44

By this time Ball had opened the rear door and had grabbed Princess Anne by the arm saying to her (with what now seems ironic politeness), 'Please get out of the car.' With equal politeness but quite firmly, she declined, and Mark Phillips took hold of her other arm and pulled her back into the car. A virtual tug-of-war followed with Ball hanging on to one arm and Mark hanging on to the other. Mark, being stronger than Ball, and using both hands whereas Ball could use only one as he had a gun in the other, won the struggle. He pulled the Princess back into the car and slammed the door.

Rowena Brassey, the Lady-in-Waiting, had managed to open the door on her side and had crawled out to lie on the pavement. Jim Beaton had returned to the nearside rear door which had been left open by Miss Brassey.

Ball, who was remarkably calm during all this mayhem, then ordered Beaton to lay down his gun, threatening to shoot the Princess if he wasn't obeyed. Beaton had no option and in any case his weapon, a Walther PPK automatic, was jammed. 'I distinctly remember thinking at the time, "I bet someone will kick the gun on the pavement and it will work straight away and then afterwards people will say that I should have continued shooting." But no one did and the gun was later proved to be faulty.'

Jim Beaton got into the rear of the car while Ball was distracted and ended up on the floor in front of Princess Anne, and facing the rear off-side door, which by this time was closed.

Ball then produced a second gun, a .22 calibre handgun, and pointed it at the Princess saying he would shoot if the door wasn't opened. Inspector Beaton, who was already weak through loss of blood from his first wound, put his hand in front of the barrel of the gun; Ball fired and Beaton was hit again. 'I could see that he was pointing the gun right at her through the window, so I put my hand up and he shot me again. Even then there was no great pain. I knew I had been shot but it was nothing like you imagine it to be. No excruciating agony or loud bangs.'

The car door was opened and Princess Anne, though badly shaken and concerned for her bodyguard, reacted calmly and spoke to Ball directly for the first time, asking him why he wanted her. He replied, 'I'll get a couple of million.'

Both Jim Beaton and Rowena Brassey could hear the conversation, and she marvelled at the quiet, controlled manner of the Princess. She said later, 'The Princess spoke in a low tone, very calmly, trying to keep his attention.' It was a classic example of how potential victims are these days taught to behave when confronted by armed attackers.

Jim Beaton had already been wounded twice and was seriously weakened, half sitting, half lying on the floor of the Royal limousine. But he refused to abandon his Royal charge and he told Mark to release his hold on the handle of the door so that he (Beaton) could kick it open suddenly and smash the gunman with it.

He did manage to kick the door open but Ball stepped back and calmly shot Beaton for a third time. This was the most serious wound as the bullet passed into his stomach, through the intestines and pelvis, and lodged in the tissues in his left buttock. It was only by a miracle that he wasn't hit in the spine, which could have paralysed him for life.

For Jim Beaton the incident was over. He managed to stagger out of the car on to the pavement alongside St James's Park where he lay until an ambulance was able to reach him some minutes later and rush him to hospital for an emergency operation that undoubtedly saved his life.

He recalls the moments following the final shooting: 'I knew that this time I was badly hit and I felt I was going to faint, but as I fell towards the roadway my one thought was about the bloodstains on my new grey suit. I edged my way around the front of the Royal car and gently lay down on the pavement.' Then in a classic example of how not to handle a seriously wounded man, a police colleague arrived and asked Jim Beaton where he was injured. On being told 'in the abdomen' he immediately moved him to the prone position; the exact opposite of what he should have done. Then to compound the error, when the ambulance arrived, the medical attendant did precisely the same thing. By this time Jim Beaton was in agony and losing blood in enormous quantities at a rapid rate.

All this had taken less than three minutes; Alex Callendar was still sitting at the wheel with the engine running. Seeing that Jim Beaton needed help, Mr Callendar switched off the engine and started to get out of the car. Ball told him to remain where he was but the chauffeur disobeyed—and paid the penalty. As he opened the driver's door Ball shot him in the chest at point-

47

blank range. It was so sudden that Mr Callendar did not at first realize what had happened. Then when it dawned on him he said, 'Good God, I've been shot.' He fell back across the front seats, bleeding badly.

Rowena Brassey recalled that during all the gunfire it never once sounded like shooting, 'It was more like the shots you hear on television ... that sort of noise ... not like real shooting at all.' The extraordinary thing about the entire incident was that while it was happening, no one outside the car seemed to realize that anything was wrong. As Princess Anne later remarked, 'I was amazed that things were going on outside as usual, cars and taxis passing as though nothing was happening.'

But by now people were beginning to realize that something untoward was taking place. Cars had started to stop in The Mall and across the road, just outside St James's Palace, a young police constable, twenty-two-year-old Michael Hills, had heard the shots and ran to help. Seeing what he immediately recognized as a Royal car with its smashed window, he approached Ball, ignoring the shouts of passers-by warning him that the man had a gun. Taking him by the elbow, he asked, 'What's going on?' Thereupon Ball turned and shot him in the chest, the bullet narrowly missing his liver. Badly wounded, Hills still managed to operate his personal radio and call for help, saying, 'There's been a shooting. I've been shot. Royal car involved. Man with gun.' He gave the location of the incident and within minutes the area was flooded with police cars, but not before there were more people involved and further shooting.

A taxi, carrying the well-known Fleet Street

journalist Brian McConnell as its passenger, had been driving down The Mall and was some thirty yards in front of the Royal car when the first shots were fired. McConnell called to the taxi driver to stop and got out and ran back. Without knowing who was in the car (the first time he met a member of the Royal Family was when Princess Anne came to see him in hospital a few days later), he approached the gunman and said, 'Look old man, these are friends of mine. Give me the gun.' Ball waved him away shouting, 'Keep out of this.' McConnell, very bravely, kept coming forward, and Ball shot him in the chest. He said later, 'Although the bullet cut a line across the front of my body, it missed all the clockwork.' But of course he did not know this at the time as he staggered to the pavement, another casualty waiting for aid.

Cars were now piling up around the scene. A Jaguar, a Mini, several taxis and police cars were all stopped as a traffic jam built up behind. The driver of the Jaguar, Glanmore Martin, had seen the incident in his rear-view mirror and, with great presence of mind, he quickly reversed his car in front of Ball's Escort, cutting off his escape route. He got out of his car and approached Ball, who ordered him to 'Clear off', pointing a gun at him as he did so. Martin could see Police Constable Hills trying to get to his feet and attempting to fire Jim Beaton's jammed gun. Seeing that Hills was obviously badly wounded, Martin supported him and managed to drag him to safety with the Royal car between them and Ball.

Another witness was a young dancing instructress, Samantha Scott. She had been driving home along The Mall in her Mini and had been forced to swerve violently when Ball stopped the Princess's car. Later she gave her version of what happened: 'I stopped my Mini and ran to the Royal car. We huddled on the ground. Inside I could see Mark Phillips on top of his wife, protecting her while the man tried to get them. I could see yellow roses scattered all over the floor ... When the gunman had gone, I opened the car door and put my hand on Anne's shoulder. I said to her, "Are you all right, love?" She replied sweetly, "I'm all right, thank you." I then asked Mark if he was OK and he said, "I'm fine, thank you."'

Rowena Brassey said later that Mark was the luckiest man not to have been shot. He had been shielding Princess Anne and, 'There were so many bullets flying around in such a confined space that it's amazing he wasn't hurt.'

Brian McDermott, an actor who had appeared in many dramas, was about to feature in a real-life incident far beyond any of those fictional episodes. Describing the event, he said, 'Suddenly I found myself in the middle of chaos ... it looked like Northern Ireland. I saw this girl ducking from the gunfire. At the same time there was fighting going on on the pavement. Then there were sirens blaring and police all around The Mall.'

In the meantime, more help was coming from passersby. Ronald Russell, an office cleaning manager, also realized something was wrong. Driving his own car close to the Royal limousine, he dashed out and saw Ball trying to wrench open the Princess's door. Russell, who is over six feet tall and well built, punched Ball on the side of the head. Ball turned and fired at him but missed. Russell ran round to the pavement and saw the carnage there with two police officers lying wounded, Rowena Brassey crouched on the ground, the journalist, Brian McConnell, also shot and bleeding, and Alex Callendar sprawled across the front seats of the car. Ball then fired off two more shots and succeeded in opening the rear door again. Starting to panic, he grabbed Princess Anne, shouting, 'Come on, Anne, you know you've got to come.' The Princess, with Mark hanging on to her other arm, replied, 'Why don't you go away? What good is this going to do?' Ball hesitated, the Princess seized her chance and twisted out of his grasp, and Russell, by now alongside Ball, nearly knocked him out with a massive punch to the head. At last, Ball, realizing his chance was gone, gave up and ran off into St James's Park. He was chased by an unarmed detective, Peter Edwards, who brought him down with a flying tackle and arrested him. It was an action that was to bring Edwards an immediate reward as he was promoted from Temporary Detective Constable to Detective Constable that same night. What could have been the crime of the century had failed. It was all over by 7.50, the entire incident, in which four people had been shot, lasting less than ten minutes. But the aftermath would be felt for many years.

The injured men were taken to hospital where they all underwent emergency operations; Jim Beaton and Alex Callendar to the Westminster, and Brian McConnell and PC Hills to St George's Hospital at Hyde Park Corner (now the Lanesborough Hotel). A police car took Anne, Mark and Rowena Brassey on to Buckingham Palace, and the blood-splattered and wrecked Royal limousine was left where it was until the

51

Home Secretary, Roy (now Lord) Jenkins, arrived to inspect the scene of the crime. When the car was being inspected by forensic experts they noticed a bump in the front off-side wing which couldn't be explained. Jim Beaton had the answer, 'When we arrived in the City for the film show, Alex Callendar drove the Austin Princess on to the pavement to park. Unfortunately he didn't see a concrete stanchion that had been put there just to stop anyone parking. As he tried to park the car he hit the post and damaged the front wing. He was worried that Princess Anne would see it when she came out, so I told him I would stand in front and hide the damage. As it happened that turned out to be the least of our problems.'

The Home Secretary had interrupted a debate in the House of Commons to tell the stunned Members of Parliament, 'I regret to have to report that an attempt was made by an armed man to kidnap Princess Anne at 8 p.m. this evening ... The attempt did not succeed. Neither Princess Anne nor Captain Phillips was hurt. I much regret to say, however, that Princess Anne's protection officer sustained very severe injuries and her driver, a police constable and a member of the public were also seriously hurt'.

Inside the Palace, both Anne and Mark were able to give detailed accounts of the incident to Scotland Yard Deputy Assistant Commissioner John Gerrard, who explained that, although they were badly shaken by the episode, it was important that their stories should be told as soon as possible after the event, before their memories of the evening clouded.

Later, the Princess telephoned her parents who

were on a State Visit to Indonesia. It was five o'clock in the morning there but Anne was anxious that her mother and father should hear the news directly from her and not pick it up from the radio the next morning. Prince Philip, once he had been reassured that all was well with his daughter, woke the Queen to tell her what had happened. Next to be informed was Prince Charles, who was in the United States where his ship, HMS *Jupiter*, was paying a courtesy call in San Diego, California.

Once the family duty calls had been made and they had been reassured about the condition of the people who had been injured, Anne and Mark decided to continue with their original plan to spend the night at their own home at Sandhurst. As they both had their cars with them, they travelled separately but in convoy, with Mark leading in his Rover 2000, followed by Anne driving herself in her Reliant Scimitar sports saloon. This time, though, they were escorted by detectives from Scotland Yard's Special Branch who were taking no chances in case Ball might have been part of a gang that might try again. The IRA issued a statement denying any involvement and no other organization claimed responsibility either. The Prime Minister, Harold Wilson, ordered an immediate inquiry, and Police Commissioner Robert Mark assigned three of his most senior officers, all Deputy Assistant Commissioners, to lead the investigation.

At first Ian Ball refused to give the police any details about himself. It was only when they established his identity through his fingerprints that he owned up and began speaking freely about his intentions. He confirmed that he had acted alone and was not part of any organization. He also showed no remorse or sympathy for the men he had shot. It emerged that Mark Phillips had been very lucky to escape injury in his efforts to safeguard his wife. Ball would have shot him out of hand if it had enabled him to get hold of the Princess more easily. He told the police, 'I didn't want him. I only wanted to take her. I thought it up a long time ago, before the wedding. In fact the wedding made me think of giving it up. They looked such a nice couple.'

The ransom note had been found on Ball when he was arrested. It was addressed to The Queen and was frighteningly explicit:

Your daughter has been kidnapped—the following conditions to be fulfilled for her release. A ransom of £3 million is to be paid in £5 notes. They are to be used, unmarked, not sprayed with any chemical substance and not consecutively numbered. The money is to be packed in 30 unlocked suitcases clearly marked on the outside. The following documents are to be prepared: a free pardon to cover the kidnapping, and anything connected with it, i.e. the possession of firearms or the murder of any police officer, a free pardon for any offences committed by myself from parking to murder. As the money is to be banked abroad, I shall be asking for a free pardon to run indefinitely for being in contravention of the Exchange Control Act. Documents are to be prepared for a civilian action to be taken against the police if they disclose my true identity, with damages of not less than £1 million. A civilian action to be taken against you or your consorts if you reveal my true identity. No excuses will be accepted for failing to compile these documents. If they cannot be drawn up under existing laws, the laws must be changed.

The lengthy letter went on to explain how the ransom money was to be delivered to Ball personally on an aircraft that was to be waiting on the tarmac at Heathrow Airport, ready for immediate take-off to Zurich. The demands continued: the transaction was to be handled personally by a Mr Clarke, one of Ball's solicitors, and even detailed what should happen if Clarke was ill, or dead. 'No one else will be acceptable. If he is ill, I want him brought to me on a stretcher. If he is dead, I want his body dug up and brought to the plane.'

The demands became more and more bizarre. The Queen was to go and see Ball herself and give him a sample signature so that he could be sure that she really was the Queen. Finally, he wrote that once he was safely in Switzerland, the aircraft could return to London and Princess Anne would be released.

Apart from the ransom note, Ball also had £700 in cash on him when he was arrested, but nothing that could reveal his identity. The day after his arrest, he appeared before a special court in London, charged with the attempted kidnapping of Princess Anne plus two further charges of attempted murder and another two of wounding. He was remanded in custody, and the following week, on 28 March, in another court appearance, one of his solicitors said, 'It should be known in the interests of the defendant and the public generally that the defendant has a confirmed history of psychiatric illness. He was diagnosed in hospital in 1967 as a schizoid and he is being examined at the moment by eminent psychiatrists.'

Ball was again remanded, for a further two months, and on 22 May, after a brief trial at which he pleaded guilty to all the charges, he was ordered to be detained indefinitely in a special hospital under the Mental Health Act. He was then taken to the top-security Rampton Hospital in Nottinghamshire where he remains to this day.

When Jim Beaton was rushed to Westminster Hospital for emergency surgery he was still conscious, so just before he was given a general anaesthetic he wished the surgeon 'Good Luck'. It was, apparently, the wrong thing to say. 'I thought I was being friendly, but he just blew up, telling me that he and his team were highly trained professionals and luck did not come into it.' Just the sort of thing to make a seriously wounded man feel relaxed before a major operation.

Two days later, Princess Anne visited Jim Beaton to thank him for saving her life. What she actually said remains a secret between them and neither is inclined to reveal the contents of what was a very private and personal conversation. But her words obviously made a deep impression and he remembers them verbatim even after twenty-four years.

Anne Beaton, Jim's wife, was at home when she heard about the incident in a television news flash. 'At first it didn't register that Jim was involved, but within minutes someone turned up to take me to Westminster Hospital and I knew he was seriously hurt. Every policeman's wife knows the feeling that when her husband goes out he could be injured or even killed, but when it happens to you, you feel strangely calm, almost as if you were waiting for it and now it's here you can deal with it.'

All those injured in the incident made full recoveries and in August of that year, just five months after being shot, Jim Beaton returned to his duties as Princess Anne's bodyguard. He remained with her until 1979 when he decided to leave the Royalty Protection Department. But four years later he was persuaded to return—in the top job—as personal police officer to the Queen, in the rank of Superintendent. He held that position for nine years before retiring as Chief Superintendent in 1992, to become Head of Security for one of the world's leading oil companies, ELF, in his home town of Aberdeen.

All those who had played a part in attempting to protect the Princess were subsequently rewarded by the Queen. Eight months after it was all over, Her Majesty held a special investiture at Buckingham Palace followed by a reception for all the men and women concerned and their families. Inspector Beaton, who had received the worst injuries, was awarded the George Cross, the highest award possible for bravery in civilian life. He was accompanied by his wife, Anne, and his two daughters, Linda and Shona, who were all presented to the Queen on this memorable day for the Beaton family.

Constable Michael Hills and Ronald Russell received the George Medal, while three others, Brian McConnell, chauffeur Alexander (Reg) Callendar and Detective Constable Peter Edwards, were all given the Queen's Gallantry Medal.

Glanmore Martin received The Queen's Commendation for Brave Conduct. Princess Anne had earlier been created a Dame Grand Cross of the Royal Victorian Order (DCVO) in recognition of her brave behaviour during the ordeal, while Mark Phillips was made a Commander of the Order (CVO) and Rowena Brassey became a Member (MVO).

In a comment made some time after the event, Mark Phillips summed up the feelings of those involved when he said: 'The moment help arrived I really thought that was it. With all the blue lights flashing, it was like cornering an animal. He could see there was no escape and at that moment I really thought we would be shot.'

One direct result of the kidnapping attempt was a complete review of the security arrangements concerning the Royal Family. Until then, although they had all had personal bodyguards, the main task had been to act as extra attendants, carrying umbrellas, folding rugs over the Royal knees and shielding their principals from the overzealous attentions of the media. From now on, all that would change dramatically. Never again would there be any excuse for a Royal bodyguard's gun to jam, or for a Royal car to be unescorted. The Walther PPK hand-gun was discarded immediately, to be replaced by a revolver, and the official weapon of the Royal bodyguards is now a Glock semi-automatic pistol, which has rarely been known to jam.

The Royal Protection Department was enlarged, with every member of the Royal Family being allocated a team of specialists to guard them around the clock. The men and women employed were all trained marksmen and experts in unarmed combat, and their training is continuous. For example, the Princess Royal has four police officers attached to her permanently and they take it in turns to attend refresher courses at the Special Air Service headquarters in Hereford in order to keep up to date with the latest techniques. The Princess Royal herself, and her Ladies-in-Waiting, have also visited Hereford to be taught the basics of self-defence and also how to act in the event of being taken hostage.

The SAS keeps detailed photographs of every room in every Royal residence so that, should a terrorist attack take place, they can go in under cover of darkness or smoke bombs and be familiar with the placing of furniture and fittings. For this reason nothing is ever moved in any of the rooms without the security forces being informed. Panic buttons are located in all principal rooms (when Prince William was very young he caused great confusion at Kensington Palace by pressing the panic buttons at regular intervals) and Royal cars are fitted with electronic homing devices so that they can be easily tracked if they deviate from their agreed route.

The Queen was involved in all the discussions that took place about the need for increased security, but in spite of the obvious dangers, she was determined that the Royal Family would not live their lives in a bulletproof cage. In this decision she was fully supported by her family, but tragically in 1979 one of them paid the ultimate price for enjoying as normal a life as possible. On August Bank Holiday Monday, Prince Philip's uncle, Earl Mountbatten of Burma, was sailing in

Mullaghmore Bay in Eire, when the IRA detonated a bomb aboard his yacht, killing him immediately, together with his fourteen-year-old grandson, a young boy helping with the boat and the Dowager Lady Brabourne, the eighty-three-year-old mother-in-law of Lord Mountbatten's elder daughter, Patricia.

Then, in 1981, a man fired a pistol containing blank cartridges at the Queen from a distance of just a few feet as she rode along The Mall to the Trooping the Colour ceremony. It could so easily have been a tragedy.

The following year Her Majesty suffered from the worst lapse of security there has ever been at Buckingham Palace when she woke to find a man, Michael Fagan, sitting on the end of her bed. He had broken into the Palace and simply walked around until he found her bedroom where the police sergeant whose task was to sit outside her door all night, had slipped away for a moment. There was confusion later over the reason for his absence, whether it was simply to have a cup of tea, or to take Her Majesty's corgis for a walk. Whatever the reason, the Queen was left unguarded and an intruder gained access to what most people would have considered the most secure room in the land.

Other members of the Royal Family have suffered from the attentions of stalkers from time to time, and the Princess Royal has herself had to put up with several unwelcome pests. On one occasion a man used to hang around the Palace gates hoping to catch a glimpse of her and would turn up at practically all her public engagements. He even found the address of one of her Ladies-in-

Waiting and arrived on the doorstep demanding to speak to the lady about the Princess. Finally, the police took him in and advised him firmly to forget his ambitions regarding the Princess Royal. He took the hint, and they took no further action, apart from noting his name in case any more complaints were forthcoming.

In January 1996, the Princess herself noticed another man whose face had become a little too familiar when she appeared in public, and informed the police. The man persisted in following her and was arrested and charged with a breach of the peace. However, the magistrate, in his wisdom, decided there was no case to answer and the man was released, but not before he had told the police that he wanted a relationship with the Princess and that he had once crashed his car while having a fantasy about having sexual relations with her. His family revealed that he had given up his job to follow the Princess everywhere and that she had become an obsession with him. There was never any suggestion that he intended her any harm, but no woman, Royal or otherwise, likes to think she is being followed by someone so besotted that his attentions might become sinister.

Certainly, in an age when people can become famous—or notorious—just for a momentary act involving a famous personality—the Pope, American Presidents and pop stars like John Lennon—it would be all too easy to attack a prominent member of the Royal Family just for the publicity. As the Princess Royal has said herself, 'You cannot live your life constantly looking over your shoulder. If someone is determined enough, an attack is virtually impossible to prevent.' And from her own personal experience on that March night in 1974, she should know.

Talking about the incident recently, Jim Beaton said that the Princess behaved impeccably and handled the affair in a classic, textbook fashion. 'She was calm, fully in control, not for one moment did she show any sign of fear or panic—and, more importantly, neither did she do or say anything to upset Ball. That was most important as we did not know his temperament or state of mind. The slightest thing could have tipped the balance and the way in which Her Royal Highness acted was the perfect example of how to conduct yourself in such a situation. Mark was also very brave and did everything he could to protect his wife in very difficult and dangerous circumstances.'

Prince Philip neatly summed up his feelings about the attempted kidnap of his daughter, when he said later that he felt rather sorry for Ian Ball, as Princess Anne would have made life somewhat difficult for any would-be abductor, adding, 'If only he had known what he was getting into.'

CHAPTER FIVE

A VERY CIVILIZED DIVORCE

Royal divorces have long been a matter of national importance. When Princess Margaret, the Queen's sister, was divorced from Lord Snowdon in 1978, the leaders of every Commonwealth country were informed officially before the news was announced in the press.

The climate of opinion had changed dramatically by the time the Queen's only daughter, the Princess Royal, was divorced from Captain Mark Phillips on 23 April 1992. The whole thing was over in just a few minutes, and although the news was given front-page status in practically every newspaper in the country, and in many abroad, officially it caused barely a ripple. No constitutional issues were raised by the divorce; the Princess was already so far removed from the possibility of inheriting the Crown that although the Commonwealth leaders were informed of the event, this was more a courtesy than a requirement.

The Queen was consulted about the divorce but it was not necessary for her to give her permission. Under the Royal Marriages Act 1771, the Sovereign's consent is required for the marriage of any of the lineal descendants of George II, but there is no rule governing divorce. Nevertheless, when Princess Anne told her mother of her intention to divorce Mark, it was not merely a courtesy; had any serious objections been raised by the Queen, much further thought and discussion would have been necessary before the final, irrevocable decision was taken, and acted upon.

The Queen had cause later that year to describe 1992 as her *annus horribilis*, for it not only saw the divorce of her only daughter, but the split in the marriage of the Prince and Princess of Wales was revealed for the first time by the publication of a book with which the Princess had cooperated. Then came the disclosure of the Duchess of York's involvement with her financial adviser, John Bryan, when pictures of her, topless, were published, and finally, to cap a decidedly unpleasant year, fire destroyed a major part of Windsor Castle. The only bright spot in an otherwise black period was the remarriage at the end of the year of the Princess Royal to Tim Laurence.

The Princess Royal was granted her divorce from Mark Phillips in the briefest of court hearings in London, which neither attended and which was witnessed by only five people: two reporters, two other women whose names were also on the list for divorces, and a lawyer representing the Princess. It was a normal day in Court Three of Somerset House, with twenty-nine similar cases disposed of in under two hours.

The Royal divorce hearing was listed as Her Royal Highness Anne Elizabeth Alice Louise, The Princess Royal, GCVO, FRS, *v* Phillips, Mark Anthony Peter. The decree nisi, unopposed by Mark, was granted in less than four minutes, paving the way for the divorce decree to be made absolute six weeks later. As the couple had lived apart for more than the requisite two years, this was accepted as proof that the marriage had broken down irretrievably. There was no guilty party—it was simply an admission by both sides that there was nothing left of their eighteen-year marriage.

Nevertheless, it was still only the fifth Royal divorce in nearly 500 years, the first being when Henry VIII divorced Catherine of Aragon some 445 years earlier, and the second when he got rid of Anne of Cleves in the same way in 1540. The third, and first this century, was when the Queen's cousin Lord Harewood was divorced in 1967, followed by that of Princess Margaret and Lord Snowdon in 1978, also after eighteen years of marriage.

Princess Anne did not even take a day off work

64

as the divorce proceedings progressed. For her it was a case of business as usual. She opened a St John Ambulance headquarters in Alton, Hampshire, visited a lemur house at nearby Marwell Zoo, and attended the launch of a sail training ship at Lymington. And when she was invited to unveil a plaque at a Citizens' Advice Bureau in Hampshire, she even joked about her new status, saying 'No strings attached' as she pulled the cord.

Her divorce was highly civilized, and remarkably amicable considering the rumours and stories that had been circulating for months in the Press before the legal separation. At the time of the divorce, Buckingham Palace had said that no third party was involved, despite the fact that Tim Laurence had admitted writing personal letters to the Princess Royal that were later stolen. The theft sparked off a spate of reports speculating about their relationship. It was really Tim's own fault that the story came out, as he openly admitted, without being pressed, that he was the author of the letters. It was the sort of break that journalists pray for, but Tim Laurence has now learnt his lesson and since then has kept his lips firmly sealed. These days he never speaks to anyone from the media—on any subject.

Mark Phillips's name had been linked with a number of women in diferent parts of the world. He had been involved in a paternity suit by Heather Tonkin, a New Zealand teacher. She alleged that she had conceived his child during a one-night stand at an hotel in Auckland in November 1984 and that he had admitted that the child—a girl—was his by the fact that he had already paid her some £40,000 in maintenance money. There was no dispute over the payment of the money, except that Mark's lawyers claimed that it was for equestrian fees. Eventually the paternity suit was dropped without it going to court, and Mark never admitted publicly that he had an illegitimate daughter.

The Palace statement that no one else was involved in the Phillipses' divorce was made less than a month before the Princess was photographed publicly with Tim Laurence for the first time. In May 1992 they attended the Caledonian Ball at London's Grosvenor House together, by which time Tim had already ordered an engagement ring from his jeweller in Winchester. If it was true that Princess Anne and Tim Laurence had no serious intentions at the time of her divorce, theirs must have been a truly lightning courtship. The Princess had accepted Tim's proposal by the time they attended the Caledonian Ball; the Queen's approval must have been sought and granted, and all this in the space of just three weeks?

The saga of the stolen love letters did of course begin much earlier and revealed that the relationship had blossomed at least three years before the divorce. It was in April 1989 that the existence of the letters first emerged when four handwritten documents were handed in to the offices of the *Sun* newspaper. At that time nobody outside Court circles had ever heard of Tim Laurence but once the authenticity of the letters and the identity of the author had been established beyond all doubt, he quickly became public property. The editor of the *Sun* decided not to publish the letters and handed them over to the police.

Scotland Yard were called in to investigate the theft and every member of the Princess's staff was fingerprinted and interviewed. At first there was some doubt about where the letters had disappeared. It might have been Buckingham Palace, Gatcombe or any of the Royal residences the Princess Royal visits. Eventually it was established that they were taken from her briefcase while she was at Windsor Castle.

On 15 April, one week after the theft had been reported, Buckingham Palace named Tim Laurence as the author and Mark Phillips was understandably furious at being made a laughing stock. The Palace had apparently thought it unnecessary to inform him about Tim's involvement, or that they were going to issue a statement. They apparently believed (wrongly) that a Sunday newspaper was about to reveal Tim as the writer, and at 11 p.m. on the Saturday night, in an attempt to pre-empt the newspapers, they announced: 'The stolen letters were addressed to the Princess Royal by Lt Cdr Timothy Laurence, the Queen's Equerry . . .'. Such lack of courtesy by the Press Office was inexcusable and Mark's anger perfectly justified as it placed him in an acutely embarrassing position, revealing to the world that Anne was having a relationship with another man while still married to him.

A number of Palace staff came under suspicion for the theft, and several were interviewed by the police. The letters, which covered a two-year period, were handed to a *Sun* reporter by a man in his twenties who refused to give his name. The four white envelopes were marked 'Private' and were addressed to the Princess Royal. The man did not wear gloves so presumably his fingerprints were on the envelopes. He obviously did not fear being found out. The Queen let it be known that she did not want a prosecution with the attendant publicity, and in May 1992 the police closed the case on the grounds that there was insufficient evidence to charge anyone with the theft.

Whoever the thief was, he or she did not do it for money, which is the usual motive, as the *Sun* was not asked for a penny. The only conclusion one can draw is that it was done out of pure malice. Someone wanted to seriously embarrass the Princess Royal, and could not have done so more successfully. Even without any revelation of the intimate contents of the letters, the very fact of their existence was enough to cause grave concern at the Palace, and what the letters did prove was that Tim Laurence and the Princess had been seeing each other for some years while she was still married to Mark Phillips. A neighbour of Tim's in Winchester, Mrs Irene Steele, confirmed this when she said, 'I saw Princess Anne going in two years ago and I've seen her in the area quite a lot since.'

The immediate reaction among Tim Laurence's colleagues at the Palace was one of horror and anger. He was ordered to remain at home and not accompany the Queen to a number of engagements he had been scheduled to attend. He was summoned by a furious Sir William Heseltine, the Queen's Private Secretary, who told him in no uncertain terms what he thought of his behaviour, only to have to climb down rapidly when he learned that the Queen had given Tim her full support.

Divorce had proved to be the great leveller for the Princess, who had to fill in a standard affidavit form just like anybody else. She signed the final petition papers at Heathrow Airport, witnessed by a solicitor, James Bacon. The petition stated that by the time the couple had separated, in September 1989, 'We had both come to the conclusion that the marriage had come to an end.' By coincidence, the declaration was signed on her mother's sixty-sixth birthday, not the happiest of presents from a dutiful daughter.

The divorce did nothing to damage the Princess's reputation; she carried on with her public duties as if nothing had happened and her image was not even dented by the break-up. Newspapers, including the *Daily Mirror*, reported that 'the public will approve because they respect her so much and because she has served her country so well'.

On the day of the hearing Tim Laurence was diplomatically absent from his desk at the Ministry of Defence, said to be on leave, sailing in the Solent near his Hampshire home. For him it meant an end to months of having to hold his meetings with the Princess in secret. They would now be able to continue their relationship in the open, even if for the next year they would be dogged continually by the Press, all anxious to catch them in an indiscreet moment. They were to be unlucky. Tim may have been inexperienced at dealing with the media but his wife-to-be was far too old a hand at avoiding tricky situations to be caught out doing something she wanted kept private.

Buckingham Palace continued to insist that the couple had no marriage plans and that Tim did not figure in the Princess's long-term future. They were able to say this because they simply had not been told about the planned wedding. The Royal Family often does this in personal matters so that the Press Office is not put in the position of having to lie. Privately, many people in the Royal Household knew what was happening and that an engagement was imminent, but publicly they were able to state, quite truthfully, that they knew of no such plans.

For years prior to the Phillipses' separation there had been rumours about the state of their marriage. Mark's reluctance to get involved in Royal duties, his long absences overseas on his many business commitments, and the Princess's equally long and frequent trips abroad meant that they spent far less time together than the average married couple of their generation. Inevitably, stories leaked out about their friendships with others; Mark's with a variety of good-looking and available women and the Princess's with a number of elegant handsome men such as the actor Anthony Andrews. In fact Andrews was a friend of both Anne and Mark and so was his wife Georgina, who had introduced him to the Princess.

When the separation was officially announced on 31 August 1989, there were those who claimed to have known all along that it was bound to happen because the marriage was a misalliance right from the start. She was a Royal through and through and he was a boy from the backwoods. This was arrant nonsense. Mark Phillips comes from a background that should have made him far more suitable as a Royal bridegroom than Tim Laurence. His grandfather, Brigadier Tiarks, was an Aide de Combat to the Queen's father, King

George VI, so accusations that Mark was unsuited to Court life or what passed for high society could not have been wider of the mark.

The problem with the marriage was that the couple simply grew apart. Mark was determined right from the start to be his own man: he did not want to be seen as a Royal hanger-on. And while he is a shy, reserved person who does not sparkle with strangers, he has been grossly maligned, mostly by those who have never met him. He is not slow-witted and it is untrue that within the Royal Family he was known as 'Fog' because he was 'thick and wet'. Mark is a decent man with a genius for handling horses and an amazing capacity for hard work. In private he is a congenial companion and loyal friend. Like the Princess, he has not been harmed by the divorce. He still moves mainly in the equestrian world where such minor domestic adjustments are taken in their stride, and his circle of friends has remained basically the same as it was when he was married to the Princess.

When the rumours were finally confirmed and the long-awaited official statement of the couple's separation was at last released by the Buckingham Palace Press Once, it was in typically terse terms: 'Her Royal Highness the Princess Royal and Captain Mark Phillips have decided to separate on terms agreed between them. There are no plans for divorce proceedings.' This last sentence was both unnecessary and untrue. The separation was planned in the full knowledge that a divorce would eventually follow, and in denying that such was the case, the Palace only succeeded in helping to fuel the cynicism with which the press and, increasingly, the general public, greet such statements. After all, what was the point of Anne and Mark going public about the breakdown of their marriage, with all the attendant publicity for themselves and their children, if they had no intention of making the split final and legal in due course? They could just as easily have continued living as they had for some years past, with Mark concentrating on his business career and the Princess following her own interests. They rarely saw each other, their paths did not regularly cross, there was little animosity. In fact it was a comfortable lifestyle and they had been separated in all but name for a number of years. So if neither party wanted the opportunity of remarrying in the foreseeable future, why bother to change their situation? The truth of the matter is that the Princess is a remarkably honest woman and when she realized that there was no possibility of their getting back together again as a married couple, that all love between them had died, and the marriage was well and truly over, she wanted out. She refused to live a sham; she wanted her freedom, and even though Mark was prepared to carry on as before, it was her decision to call it a day. He did not fight the decision and they both knew that after the separation, a divorce would follow.

The timing of the announcement of the separation had been planned many months in advance and if all had gone according to plan, the Princess would have been shielded from any intrusive questions from the media. But a leak to a tabloid newspaper threw the arrangements into confusion.

The original intention was to release the official statement at 11 a.m. on Thursday, 31 August 1989.

Robin Janvrin, at that time the Queen's Press Secretary, now Her Majesty's Deputy Private Secretary, was charged with the responsibility. If things had gone as intended, the Princess would have been safely ensconced at the time behind the security fences at a British Army base in Belize where nobody from the Press would have been able to get anywhere near her. But owing to a lucky break of the sort that journalists dream of, James Whitaker of the *Daily Mirror*, one of the most experienced Royal reporters in the world, got the scoop that would make front-page news in the next morning's edition of his newspaper, closely followed by every other paper.

Major Peter Phillips, Mark's father, at home in the village of Great Somerford in Wiltshire, inadvertently let the cat out of the bag when, believing the story had already been released, he confirmed the details, saying that he was 'very sad' at the collapse of his son's marriage. It was a perfectly natural reaction and, of course, there was no intention on the Major's part of leaking the story, he merely assumed from the skilful questioning that the news was out. In fact no great harm was done. It just upset the carefully laid plans of Buckingham Palace who like to manage these things to suit themselves.

Mark Phillips was en route home from Canada when the story broke and the Princess was about to enter a meeting of the International Olympic Committee in Puerto Rico. She refused to answer any questions about the separation but it was one of the few occasions when the Buckingham Palace news management system went wrong. Instead of being protected on an Army base, she was exposed—for a few hours at least—to the world's media. She was not a happy woman.

If the public and the media expected separation and divorce to make a significant difference to the way in which the Princess organized her life, they were to be disappointed. Her reaction to events was to behave as if nothing had happened. She carried on exactly as she had before and provided a classic example of how to deal with what for most people is a traumatic emotional experience, by simply ignoring it. There was no period of hiding away from the public gaze and hoping the attention would go away. Nor did she seek to put her side of the story or justify her actions. As far as she was concerned it was an episode in her life that was over and done with and she saw no point in discussing it with anyone. The decision had been made; if there was any private torment or doubt about the split, all had been resolved far away from the public's attention long before the news was released.

Mark, too, had taken a vow never to speak about his marriage or its break-up, and he never has. Just as Princess Margaret and Lord Snowdon, albeit at a time when there was less tabloid press intrusion, felt the least said the better, Anne and Mark believed that the best way to deal with the end of their marriage was to say nothing. They have since been proved absolutely right, as the Prince and Princess of Wales and the Duchess of York have found to their cost. If you say nothing, at least your own words cannot come back to haunt you.

On the question of divorce generally within the Royal Family, the Princess Royal restricts her comments—at least those which are for public, if

74

limited, hearing—to saying it is the business only of those involved. Privately, though, she is known to consider the actions of both her married brothers, Charles and Andrew, as inexplicable and unnecessary. As both are so closely positioned to the throne, she feels they should have thought long and hard before making any decisions that could have constitutional implications. Regarding her own divorce, she knows that she was, and is, so unlikely to inherit the crown that the divorce was merely a personal matter. And while it is known that the Queen and the Duke of Edinburgh were both deeply saddened by the affair, they agreed that the divorce could take place without it having any major impact on the Monarchy. If the Princess had thought for one moment that by divorcing when she did, she would have harmed either her family or the institution of the Monarchy, she would not have proceeded. With her duty comes before all else, including her own happiness, and she would have maintained the status quo if she or the Queen had felt it was necessary to the well-being of the Crown.

Peter and Zara Phillips had been told of their parents' plans long before the separation became public knowledge and they reacted with what in these days is fairly typical equanimity. They knew there was no question of their not being able to see both parents whenever they wished, and as a teacher at Peter's school remarked: 'He is now part of the majority. Two-thirds of the pupils in the school are from broken homes.' So the break-up did not make a great deal of difference to either child and that had been the main concern of both Mark and the Princess. Equally they came to terms fairly quickly with their new stepfather—they call him Tim—and while Peter remains very much his father's son, with Zara her mother's favourite, they both seem to regard Tim as an older brother or uncle.

Domestically, the Laurences and Phillipses appear to have resolved their family difficulties to everyone's satisfaction. Nobody appears to have been hurt by the divorce, and again nobody could accuse the Princess Royal of not trying with her first marriage. Eighteen years is a long time, so there was no question of her rushing to get out of it. She reflected long and hard before taking her decision and once she had decided that divorce was the only answer she behaved with dignity and courtesy towards her estranged husband.

Not many couples can honestly claim to remain as friendly as Anne and Mark have, and this must be seen as a tribute to the people they are and the common bond they still share through their children. There is no bitterness between them and when Mark was told about the impending marriage of his ex-wife he wished them both the best of luck—and he meant it! He still lives on the Gatcombe Park estate, occupying Aston Farm adjoining Gatcombe itself. He received the tenancy as part of the divorce settlement, while Tim Laurence has settled in as the new master at the big house. Mark sees his two children whenever he wants; he even goes shooting with his former wife's new husband. The marriage may be over but a great deal of mutual respect remains between these two highly independent individuals.

CHAPTER SIX

TWO WEDDINGS

There could scarcely have been a greater contrast than the two weddings of the Princess Royal. Wedding number one to Mark Phillips in November 1973 took place in the grandest of English churches, Westminster Abbey, with the Archbishop of Canterbury officiating and 1600 guests attending. Months of meticulous planning and preparation for the event had involved endless meetings with representatives of the Armed Forces, Church authorities, the Foreign and Home Offices, the Metropolitan Police, the BBC, the Department of the Environment, Westminster City Council, all under the watchful eye of the Head of the Queen's Household, the Lord Chamberlain.

On 12 December 1992, the Princess married husband number two, Commander Tim Laurence, in the simplest of services that was strictly a family affair. No foreign Royalty, no show business or sports celebrities were invited, and the ceremony had been arranged with what, in Royal terms, was almost indecent haste. In fact it has even been suggested that her Royal Highness broke the law in Scotland by not giving the requisite two weeks' notice of her intention to marry. The reason for that, of course, was to try to keep it out of the papers.

The marriage took place in the tiny parish church at Crathie, just outside the gates of Balmoral Castle in the Scottish Highlands, on a bleak, wintry afternoon, and once again the Princess was notching up a first. She became the first member of the Royal Family to remarry after a divorce since Henry VIII married Anne Boleyn in 1533, after divorcing his first wife, Catherine of Aragon, the same year. Scotland was chosen to avoid any possible embarrassment to the Church of England as the Princess had so recently been divorced—the Church of Scotland does not bar divorcees from remarrying in church.

One of the people who had to keep secret for the longest time the fact that Tim Laurence and the Princess Royal were going to get married, was Carol Darby. Carol is a distinguished jeweller who had carried on her business in Winchester for more than ten years when she received her Royal commission to make both the engagement and wedding rings. She had already made various items of jewellery for a number of famous people, including several well-known actors and politicians, so she knew how to be discreet—a prerequisite for anyone hoping to obtain a member of the Royal Family as a customer. Carol had known Tim as a client for some time before he gave her the most exciting order of her business life. 'He'd been in the shop many times and my husband and I also saw him occasionally in the local wine bar on Friday evenings. But I was totally unprepared for the bombshell he dropped when he told me what it was he wanted. This was in May, seven months before the wedding, so I had quite a long time to nurse the secret. The biggest problem was not being able to tell my mother. I was dying to let her in on the secret, but I didn't dare.'

With typical Service efficiency, Tim knew exactly

what he wanted. He had measured the Princess's finger, so he knew the right size, and also which stones, metal and design he had in mind. But knowing Carol's work and reputation as he did, once he had told her his requirements he wisely left everything to her. The Princess did not accompany him to Carol's premises, indeed Carol had never met her before making the rings. She explained how the operation proceeded. 'Once Commander [as he then was] Laurence had outlined what he and the Princess had in mind, I made several drawings and submitted them to the couple. They then chose, with a couple of suggestions of their own, which ones they wanted. It was all very relaxed, Commander Laurence was a very easy client; not difficult at all. I had several ideas of my own, with four basic guidelines about the Princess Royal's needs. In the first place I had noticed that unlike most other members of the Royal Family she rarely wore jewellery, so it needed to be fairly simple. Then I thought it was important for the engagement ring to have a classical look about it as she has a very regal demeanour. Thirdly, I bore in mind that she is very much a working woman. If you look at her hands they are tremendously strong and she has obviously used them in hard physical contact of some sort. Her riding career bears this out. Finally, she is first and foremost a Princess, so I wanted the rings to complement what is, after all, her totally Royal appearance.'

Carol worked on the rings herself with the help of four others, none of whom had any idea of the identity of the client. 'Commander Laurence and the Princess had decided they wanted a fairly unusual stone; a Burmese central cabochon sapphire with a smooth dome, not faceted, which is the normal way sapphires are shown. It is an oval shape and measures some ten by eight millimetres. On each side are three diamonds in the shape of a triangle, set in white gold, while the band is of 18-carat yellow gold. The sapphire took some finding and it was a good job I had several months in hand otherwise it could have been something of a problem.'

Throughout the time that Carol Darby worked on the rings, she was not told the date of the wedding. 'In fact, it wasn't until two weeks before the ceremony that Commander Laurence told me that it was happening. I then asked him if I could tell my mother and he said it would be all right in a few days as long as no one else heard.'

Carol did not have to make a wedding band for the bridegroom. Tim told her that he knew of a naval colleague who had seriously injured his hand in an accident at sea when his wedding ring caught in a piece of machinery, so he was not going to wear one. The Princess's wedding ring was a plain gold band of 18-carat yellow gold; she had considered 22-carat but rejected it because it was too heavy.

Once the news was announced that a wedding was to take place and also who had made the rings, Carol was inundated with requests for interviews. 'I had my first, and possibly last, taste of what it's like to be a celebrity. I enjoyed it enormously but I certainly don't envy the Royal Family having to put up with it all the time. There were queues of reporters and photographers outside the shop and it was very difficult to get any work done. They all asked the same question: how much did the engagement ring cost? I told them that was a secret between me and my clients and it would be the same whoever it was, Royalty or otherwise. I simply never divulge the price that people pay. It's a private matter.'

Shortly after the wedding, Carol met her Royal client for the first time. 'Commander Laurence telephoned to say that he and his wife were going to be visiting his former house in Winchester and that the Princess would quite like to meet the person who had designed her wedding and engagement rings. I was very excited and my husband, Peter, who has been an admirer of the Princess Royal for years, said he wanted to come too. We actually had a bet about what she would be wearing. He thought it would be a formal, navy blue suit and I said it would be jeans. I won. When we got to the house they were packing up ready for Commander Laurence to move out. There were boxes everywhere and there was the Princess Royal up to her eyes in dust—wearing jeans. She was delightful, with no aloofness or anything to show she was Royal, and yet you could tell there was something different about her. Both my husband and I were so pleased that our preconceptions about her were proved to be correct. She was exactly as we had hoped.' And so Carol Darby had another satisfied customer—this time a rather special one!

If the Princess Royal's second wedding was a modest, family affair, her first had been an occasion for national celebration as the first of the Queen's children to marry set the style for her generation of Royal weddings. An estimated audience of 500 million throughout the world watched as the proceedings were televised live to 141 countries. BBC television and radio drafted in over 300 engineers, producers and commentators to capture every moment from the time the bride left Buckingham Palace to the exchange of vows before the High Altar in the Abbey.

The souvenir industry did a roaring trade with mugs, plates, tankards, tea cloths and every kind of jewellery all bearing the couple's likeness, and all carefully vetted by the Palace. It was reckoned that over £2 million worth of goods were sold in the weeks leading up to the big day. It was the biggest single consumer bonanza seen in Britain for decades with Anne-and-Mark pottery, writing paper, bookmarks—even toilet paper, though this last item was strictly pirated and had definitely not been approved by the Lord Chamberlain. A silver-gilt bride's loving cup sold out at £125, and 500 other two-handed cups sold out in the first three days. Breweries brought out special Anne-and-Mark bottles of beer to mark the occasion and the least expensive of all the souvenirs was a box of matches with the greeting 'Health and Happiness to the Bride and Groom', retailing at a halfpenny. Copies of the bride's wedding dress appeared in the shops within hours of the original being seen for the first time, and sold in their hundreds.

Wedding presents poured in from all over the world and were eventually put on exhibition in St James's Palace where they were seen by 25,000 people, the entrance fees going to the Princess's favourite charities. The presents numbered 1524 and the list containing details of each one ran to 101 pages. Every person who sent a gift received an acknowledgement and some twenty-five extra staff were hired to cope with the deluge of letters and telegrams that arrived in sackfuls. The Royal presents were headed by those of the Queen and the Duke of Edinburgh. Her Majesty gave two pairs of diamond earrings mounted in 18-carat gold, a gold stalactite brooch set with diamonds, two gold and enamel bell-pushes and a gold Patek Philippe dress pocket-watch for Mark. Prince Philip gave the couple a beautiful Chippendale mahogany writing desk, *c.* 1765. The Queen Mother gave her granddaughter a magnificent diamond tiara, while the Prince of Wales sent his sister a diamond brooch and for Mark, two leather gun-cases. Other members of the family offered more diamonds, pearls, jewellery, carpets, furniture, crystal, silver, porcelain and china. Show-jumper David Broome, an old friend of the Princess and a guest at the wedding, gave the couple a Coalport strawberry set and one little girl sent a couple of toffees.

As the Princess left Buckingham Palace for Westminster Abbey, the Royal procession was a mass of glittering spectacle. Troopers of the Household Cavalry escorted the Glass Carriage along The Mall, which was lined with soldiers and police every few yards to keep the vast crowds in check.

Almost twenty years later, the ever-practical and realistic Princess Royal displayed what must surely become the more acceptable face of modern Royal weddings. A simple notice pinned up in the local register office proclaimed this was to be Marriage No. 41; that was the only official notification of the event. For the ceremony itself there was no pomp and ceremony; no horse-drawn State carriages from the Royal Mews; not even a special wedding dress for the Royal bride. The motorcade consisted of a small fleet of dark green Range Rovers, suitably appropriate for the terrain, but perhaps also a slightly uncomfortable reminder for the Princess that this was the very company that had sponsored Mark Phillips for so many years. And where 50,000 people had lined the route in 1973, many camping out all the previous night to gain the best vantage points, now fewer than 200 braved the bitterly cold weather on that raw Scottish afternoon. The police had confidently predicted a crowd of 4,000.

The spectators were easily outnumbered by the police and Press corps who had been detailed to observe the ceremony—all of them from the outside as no provision had been made for any media to be admitted inside the church. At Westminster Abbey in 1973, the media were charged £23 each for their seats, the explanation being that special stands had to be erected to accommodate them. This time no amount of money could have bought a seat inside. Anyone who looked as if they might have even a mildly interesting story to tell was swooped upon by the waiting reporters to be interviewed. A Russian group had come over from Aberdeen where they worked for an oil company, and a Canadian lady who was such an ardent monarchist that she had flown over specially from Ontario just so she could stand for hours in the biting wind hoping to catch a glimpse of the Royal party.

The guest list at the ceremony and the reception that followed was restricted to family and close friends of the couple, and the first to arrive at the church were those on the groom's side. One group turned up in a mini-bus and sensibly remained inside with the heater turned full on until just before the Royals came over from Balmoral. The church was not heated and the less time the guests had to spend inside the more comfortable they would be.

Tim Laurence, with his best man Charles Barker-Wyatt (an old friend from university days), reached the church twenty minutes before the wedding was due to begin, and like the rest of the Royal party he came in a four-wheel-drive Land Rover Discovery. There were no limousines for the thirty-odd guests who had been invited.

Prince Andrew, without his estranged Duchess, drove the Queen and Queen Elizabeth the Queen Mother in yet another Range Rover, with Prince Charles, also minus his wife, sitting alongside him in the front passenger seat. (The Princess of Wales was already back in London, having written a personal note to Tim Laurence wishing him the best of luck in joining the Royal Family.) The bride herself, accompanied by her father, Prince Philip, and her daughter, Zara, exercised the bride's prerogative, arriving at the church some ten minutes late, shortly after 3 p.m.

It was by far the most informal Royal wedding ever. The male guests did not even wear morning dress—lounge suits and the occasional kilt (Prince Charles wore one of Balmoral tweed) were the order of the day. Commander Laurence was the most formally dressed man present, smartly turned out in his best naval uniform.

The Queen wore a bright green coat with matching hat while the Queen Mother's outfit was in her favourite shade of blue. The bride chose an ivory-coloured suit and a black hat trimmed with snow-drops, made for her by her favourite milliner, John Boyd. She also showed off for the first time her diamond and sapphire engagement ring, but no photographer managed to get close enough to see it clearly.

For such a festive occasion, nobody gave the appearance of being ecstatically happy as they entered the church. None of the Royal party waved to the waiting crowd outside, in fact they rather gave all the appearance of a family under siege, which in many ways they were, following the announcement of the separation of the Prince and Princess of Wales some days earlier. Apparently Anne had said she wanted no publicity at all and she was obviously not pleased at the extensive media presence. The attempts at privacy assumed absurd and totally unnecessary proportions when officials, presumably on the bride's orders, placed two vehicles directly across the entrance to Crathie Church in order to prevent anyone seeing the arrivals. The entire ceremony could of course have been held in complete privacy inside the Castle grounds in the private chapel, where no outsiders, media or public, would have been able to see anything at all.

One lesson the Princess had learnt from her previous marriage was not to give any television interviews before her wedding. When she and Mark had been jointly interviewed by the BBC and ITV in 1973, the result was an excruciatingly stilted and forced half-hour. It was a complete disaster, so this time there were no interviews, either with or without Tim. As she arrived at the church, the

Princess noticed a television sound engineer carrying a microphone. With her customary tact she said, 'We'll have to unplug that ... we must keep things under control ... I don't want one of those stood at the altar.'

There had been no rehearsal for the half-hour service and before they entered the church, the Princess Royal had to remind her father that he was standing on the wrong side. He quickly moved to her left as they walked up the short aisle to the altar, attended by eleven-year-old Zara. The Revd Keith Angus, Chaplain of The Queen's Household at Balmoral, conducted the service as the couple exchanged vows. The bride did not promise to obey her husband as these words are not included in the Church of Scotland version of the marriage service. They did however, promise to stay 'loving, faithful and loyal ... until God shall separate us by death'. History was being made in Crathie Church, whose foundation stone was laid by Queen Victoria in 1893. Generations of Royalty have worshipped in the church (the Royal Family has its own special pews shielded from the main congregation) but never before had a Royal wedding been celebrated there. This was yet another first for Anne as the marble busts of her ancestors, Queen Victoria, King George V and her grandfather, King George VI, looked down on this latest Royal tableau.

Thirty minutes after they had first entered the church, and almost before the watchers outside had managed to start thawing out inside their cars, the bride and groom emerged to the strains of a lone piper playing 'Mairie's Wedding'. His fee has not been revealed, but at the first wedding in Westminster Abbey members of the choir did very well out of the royalties paid for the various recordings sold around the world, each one getting around £200 for their day's work. Mark Phillips had insisted that his regimental march—of 1st The Queen's Dragoon Guards—should be played as they left the Abbey. The trouble was that the tune, 'The Radetzky March', is more suited to a cavalry trot than a stately walk down the aisle. Prince Philip was said to have remarked that they were lucky the whole family did not break into a gallop.

At her second wedding the Princess was carrying a small bouquet of lily-of-the-valley and white heather and she had placed a white shawl around her shoulders—her only concession to the icy weather—as the Queen paused long enough to chat to a group of children from the local village school. Then the unusual motorcade—four-wheel-drive Land Rovers (Tim Laurence driving his new wife and step-daughter), mini-buses and even one modest Lada—headed for the reception at Balmoral, not held at the Castle proper, which was closed for the winter, but in a servants' annexe. The newly-weds were to spend their wedding night at Craigowan, the six-bedroomed house a mile inside the estate which also happened to have been the place where Princess Anne and Mark Phillips announced their engagement.

By Royal standards the reception was a very low-key affair. In 1973 the wedding breakfast was held at Buckingham Palace with 120 guests present including visiting Royalty, family and close friends. The menu was a comparatively modest three-course meal, beginning with scrambled eggs, lobster, shrimps and tomato in mayonnaise, then a main course of partridge with mushrooms, peas, cauliflower and new potatoes, followed by peppermint ice-cream filled with grated chocolate. (A hundred years earlier a previous Princess Royal had sat down to a fifteen-course wedding breakfast that lasted five hours.) At Balmoral, the wedding reception lasted just under an hour, and the guests enjoyed a buffet of chicken soup, a selection of sandwiches, bowls of crisps and cups of tea, though there was champagne for the toasts. And as with most weddings, Royal and non-Royal, the families of the bride and groom tended to stick with their own side. Among the guests on the Royal side were Lady Susan Hussey, one of The Queen's Ladies-in-Waiting, and her husband, former BBC Chairman 'Duke' Hussey. Lady Susan had been 'loaned' to the Princess when she was eighteen and starting out in public life. She once threatened to jump out of a car Anne was driving, if she didn't stop her flow of bad language.

Shortly after five the guests departed. The Laurences, including Tim's widowed mother and his brother Jonathan, were to catch a scheduled flight back to London, while the Royal relations had the convenience of an aircraft of what was then known as The Queen's Flight.

No one could accuse the Princess Royal of extravagance. She had certainly not caused her parents or the general public to spend large amounts of money on this wedding day. The first wedding had been a multi-million pound affair; this one cost less than £2,000.

The overall feeling was that most people were glad that the Princess had found true happiness at last. Nobody grudged her a second chance at a lasting marriage, and the form of her wedding, if

89

not exactly what many people had expected of a member of the Royal Family, was what she and Tim had wanted. It was their day, refreshingly unpretentious and as far as the two most important characters were concerned, totally sincere. They were obviously delighted with each other and completely relaxed as they enjoyed their first hours as man and wife.

It had been an unusual and slightly mystifying occasion, with the Queen's only daughter, a divorcee, marrying a former servant, and a commoner to boot, in the Scottish kirk, with the minimum of formality. Somehow, one got the impression that Queen Victoria would not have been amused.

CHAPTER SEVEN

TIM LAURENCE

When the Princess Royal married for the second time, it was to a man who fifty years ago would never have been considered as suitable husband material for the daughter of the Sovereign (any more, for that matter, than her first husband would). Tim Laurence comes from middle-class stock, with no private fortune or aristocratic pedigree. What he does possess is an intelligent and enquiring mind, ambition and integrity. He is also rising through the ranks of the Royal Navy entirely on his own merits and was marked out as a 'high-flyer' long before anyone knew of his Royal associations and his marriage to the Princess Royal

90

had catapulted him into the major league.

He was a servant of the Queen for three years after being seconded from the Royal Navy to be a personal Equerry in the Royal Household. That was how he first met the Princess, when she was still married to Mark Phillips. Completely different in temperament from Mark, Tim Laurence is the perfect partner for the Princess. He loves the Royal scene, enjoys being in the public eye, and, as a man who very quickly learned his way around Buckingham Palace, is guaranteed not to rock the boat. Where Mark went to extraordinary lengths to avoid public duties, Tim basks in the reflected glory of being—albeit only by marriage—a member of the most famous family in the world. He has quickly taken on an air of assumed aristocracy, dressing, talking and behaving just like any other Royal, no longer having to worry about looking for pubs with a 'Happy Hour'! It is a tribute to his chameleon-like qualities that he has managed to become assimilated into the Royal Family without causing a ripple. Even today, though—on the Queen's orders—the Princess Royal does not bear the name of her husband, as did the last woman to hold the title, Princess Anne's great-aunt, Princess Mary, who throughout her married life was known as HRH The Princess Royal, Countess Lascelles.

So the marriage may have been welcomed publicly as an example of how the Royal Family is becoming more democratic in its relationships, but the fact is that the Princess Royal has not in any way lowered her standards—or her attitudes. She is still as independent as she ever was, and marriage to a commoner has not in the slightest way altered her opinions about the Monarchy, or her own position.

Commander Timothy James Laurence joined the Royal Household as a complete outsider. When he was selected to become an Equerry to the Queen, his posting was unusual in that most young officers who are chosen for these highly visible and socially desirable positions come from similar backgrounds: Eton, Sandhurst and the Guards is the most conventional route by which young men find their way to Buckingham Palace. Most of them seem to know each other and their families often have connections stretching back several generations. In other words, they can be relied upon to know the form.

So Tim Laurence must have had something extra to make him stand out in this very privileged society. As a career naval officer he was one of those who were expected to reach the top without any need of special connections. A former colleague said, 'If ever a man was destined to be an Admiral, that man is Tim Laurence. He is ambitious, highly intelligent and single-minded to a degree that can be frightening.'

Andrew Parker Bowles commented, 'Being married to the Princess Royal won't help him in the slightest. Those days are long gone, in fact, some people would even mark him down because of it. Today ability is all that counts. Anyway, he doesn't need that sort of help. He was singled out for the "fast stream" as soon as he had been in the Navy for just a few years and he is obviously going to reach the top rank in the Service.'

Tim's late father, Guy, the son of a salesman, also became a Commander in the Royal Navy. When he retired, the senior Commander Laurence became a sales representative for a marine engine manufacturer.

While Tim showed considerable promise as a youngster, though without any sign of the social success that was to come later, his A-level results at Sevenoaks School—a comparatively minor if ancient public school in Kent, where he was a scholarship entrant and house captain—were not good enough to secure him a place at either Oxford or Cambridge. Instead he opted for the Royal Naval College at Dartmouth, from where he was sent on a naval scholarship to the University of Durham to read geography. Standing well over 6 feet tall, he was the tallest player in the university football squad and was considered to be a tough and aggressive opponent. Off the field, Tim made little impression on his contemporaries. 'Peculiarly unremarkable' and 'solid and reliable' were just two of the descriptions applied to him by his fellow students.

He did, however, become Secretary of the Junior Common Room and College Treasurer and, briefly in his third year, editor of the university newspaper, *Palatinate*. At this stage he acquired his college nickname, Tiger Tim, not as a reflection of his aggressive spirit or enthusiasm for crusading journalism, but for his tireless energy and for the manner in which he unrelentingly chased contributors whose copy was late.

It was at university that Tim cultivated the stiff-upper-lip persona that was to carry through to his career in the Senior Service as a member of the officer corps, and would ultimately ensure him a place in the Royal Household. He signed himself T. J. H. Laurence, and in contrast to most of his colleagues (but not all, as Durham was even then considered to be the place would-be Oxbridge undergraduates chose as their second choice) always dressed immaculately in a jacket with shirt and tie, with knife-edge creases in his trousers. This was in the seventies, when university students were notoriously anti-establishment and showed it in their manners, their speech and most of all their dress. But not so Tim Laurence. He had been brought up to have impeccable manners, and it says much for his character that, in spite of jeers and sniggers from his fellow students, he would always stand up when a woman entered the room, he would not dream of sitting down if a lady was standing on a train or bus, and he would invariably introduce himself formally to any new acquaintance. He combined old-world charm with a natural diffidence that some people found difficult to come to terms with but which others felt was a manifestation of an earlier unsureness in himself. If he did appear to be reserved, it was only with those he did not know very well, and some of the students at Durham said he was well liked and had a great sense of humour, even if he was not regarded as a great socializer.

Much later, when he was about to be married, a number of his former fellow students made predictably disparaging remarks about his joining the Royal Family. One, rather patronizingly, and with what sounded suspiciously like sour grapes, said 'I'd have thought he'd have a wife, 2.2 children, a semi in the suburbs, and a job in the City.'

After graduating from Durham in 1975 with a good degree (2.1), Tim returned to the Navy and in

1979 was appointed to the Royal Yacht *Britannia* as a Season officer. These are the youngest officers in the Yacht who join for a year—the Royal Family uses *Britannia* mainly during the summer months, and occasionally in the winter if an overseas tour is planned. The Season officers get all the worst jobs: they live in a tiny area of the Yacht which is so cramped it is known as 'The Ghetto', and if there is a particularly unpleasant job to be done the cry will go up: 'Give it to one of the Seasons—it'll do him good.' Tim was made Royal Household Liaison Officer, which sounds very grand but is in fact a sort of dogsbody whose main task is to make sure the staff from Buckingham Palace are kept happy when they are on board.

During a voyage each of the Season officers can expect to be invited to have lunch or dinner at least once with the Royal Family and Tim was no exception. The summons came via the Keeper and Steward of the Royal Apartments, who also told Tim what the dress code would be. Officers rarely know in advance when they are going to be invited to the State Apartments, so every day they 'mirror' the dress of the senior male Royal on board in order not to be caught out if a last-minute summons arrives.

Tim made the most of his brief time on the Yacht and established a number of useful connections among the Queen's Household, which would come in very handy in the years to come. He learned how to conduct himself among members of the Royal Family and impressed the Queen sufficiently for his name to be noted as a future Equerry, though it was to be another seven years before he received the summons to Buckingham

Palace that would change his life in such dramatic fashion. And it was while serving on *Britannia* that Tim first met his future wife, at that time still Mrs Mark Phillips.

After leaving the Royal Yacht he won his first naval command in 1982 when he took over the Ulster patrol boat *Cygnet*, guarding against IRA arms supply routes. He was an outstanding officer who was mentioned in dispatches, and promotions followed in rapid succession. The actions he was involved in were so successful—and secret—that even today the Ministry of Defence refuses to release any details or to discuss his part in them.

It was in 1986 that Tim Laurence joined the Queen's Household as the Sovereign's Equerry. His immediate predecessor had been Major Hugh Lindsay, a very popular Aide whose wife, the former Sarah Brennan, worked in the Palace Press Office. Major Lindsay had been skiing with the Prince of Wales in Switzerland when he was killed in an avalanche, and his untimely death caused great sadness within the Household.

Several of the young women who work at Buckingham Palace remember Tim's arrival and his initial friendliness and charm. He would occasionally drop into one of the offices on the second floor to ask one of the girls to sew on a button or help in some other way before he went into the Royal presence. He often stopped for a chat and a cup of coffee. But all this stopped within six or seven weeks of his appointment. He quickly realized his position and became more distant and formal in his relations with the officials at the Palace. It wasn't that he was particularly snobbish; it was just that he was suffering the early symptoms of what the old-timers call 'Red Carpet Fever'—the feeling that one is as Royal as the Royals. The attitude did not last long, however, and since he has become a member of the Royal Family his behaviour to his former colleagues has been impeccable. In fact, everyone seems to regard him as good news these days.

A Palace footman who acted for a time as personal valet to Tim said he was easy to work for, if slightly distant. The daily routine went as follows: the valet would enter Tim's second-floor bedroom just before seven o'clock in the morning, carrying the wake-up tray—tea or coffee and biscuits. Carrying the tray in one hand, he would then draw the curtains and switch on the radio, making sure it was tuned to BBC Radio 4, as Tim liked to hear the early morning news and the *Today* programme. The routine with other Equerries had been that the valet would not speak unless spoken to first and he would wait beside the bed until the Equerry woke up. With Tim there was no such nonsense. He was usually awake by the time the valet came in and invariably exchanged greetings in a completely informal and cheerful tone.

Next, Tim's clothes from the previous evening would be removed and a fresh set laid out. Part of the valet's job was to find out from a colleague on the Queen's personal staff what the order of that day was to be, so that he would know which uniform or suit to lay out. If there was to be an Investiture it would be full dress uniform complete with sword and decorations. If it was a normal day, but one on which Her Majesty would be granting audiences, the dress would be Number One uniform with gold braid placed over the right shoulder. If the Queen was remaining in the Palace and had no plans to see anyone, then a lounge suit would be worn by the Equerry, always with highly polished black shoes. The valet recalled that he would sponge and press all Tim's clothes every day, but that they were generally in excellent condition, and when he first arrived at Buckingham Palace, his shoes already bore the results of many hours' spit and polish.

If Tim was to be present at an evening function, a State Banquet, formal dinner or reception, his evening clothes—Mess jacket, black tie and cummerbund—were made ready and laid out for him to change into once he had bathed and shaved. According to the valet, Tim shaved twice a day, first thing in the morning and again before dinner.

It is a truism that no man is a hero to his valet, but if Tim possessed any unpleasant characteristics, he appeared to hide them well from his valet at Buckingham Palace. He was described as fastidious, neat and thoughtful, and, unlike some of his predecessors, a few of whom were said to be 'slobs' when it came to personal habits, he came as a pleasant surprise. He did not throw his clothes around, expecting someone else to pick them up after him, nor did he leave the bathroom looking as if a tornado had hit it. He was always careful to screw the top back on the toothpaste, cleaned his razor himself, and folded the bath towels neatly.

Tim displayed perfect manners towards the domestic staff but demanded perfection from them. He would not tolerate sloppiness from anyone, nor did he encourage familiarity. He was aware of his special position in relation to the Queen and made sure that others were aware of it also. He spent three Christmases with the Royal Family, staying at Windsor and Sandringham, and every year he would give a present—a bottle of whisky was usual—to the man on duty as his valet.

During the three years of his secondment Tim made himself indispensable to the Royal Family and quickly became a great favourite of the Queen and Prince Philip, and obviously, though no one knew it at the time, of the Princess Royal. She not only liked what she saw in him, but also trusted him implicitly, not something she felt with most people until she had known them for many years. But Tim was different, and in 1988 the Princess Royal invited him to become a Trustee of her private charity, The Princess Royal's Charity Trust (the other Trustees were the Queen's solicitor, Sir Matthew Farrer, and Lieutenant Colonel Peter Gibbs) as a mark of the esteem in which she held him.

It was when rumours of their relationship began to leak out that Tim's family background started to be of interest to observers. And when it was discovered that he has Jewish and Italian blood in his veins and that his family had changed their name, he became the subject of more detailed investigation.

Tim Laurence's great-great-great grandfather, Zacharia Levy, was born in Venice in 1751. A moderately successful Jewish trader, he decided to increase his fortune and try his luck in Britain and emigrated to London in the latter part of the eighteenth century. Zacharia worked hard and success followed: he became one of the first Jewish underwriters to be admitted as a member of Lloyd's, the world's foremost insurance market. His wife, Simcha Anna, whom he married in 1787, belonged to the Montefiore family which later became one of the most prominent Jewish families in Britain.

Zacharia died in London in 1828 at the age of seventy-six, survived by his wife for another ten years. His eldest son Joseph (one of nine children) was born in 1791. He married Penelope Jackson in 1813, and after her death in 1841, married the daughter of Sir Charles Rich, Bt, a union which first brought the Laurences into contact with the titled classes. Joseph carried on the family business but not the name, deciding to change his surname to Laurence in 1826, two years before his father died. He himself died in 1878, at the family home in Beddington, Surrey.

Anti-Semitism was rife in certain parts of Britain in the eighteenth and early nineteenth centuries, and the decision to change the family name from Levy to the more Saxon-sounding Laurence was probably taken for practical business reasons rather than those of an ideological or religious nature. It was certainly not unknown for Jewish businessmen in Britain to change their names at this time, but had Joseph not done so, the Princess Royal's married name today would be Mrs Timothy Levy.

It was with the next generation that the Laurence family severed all their Jewish links, when Joseph's son, Percival, born in 1829, espoused the Anglican faith and became a Church of England clergyman. He then cemented his new-found status by marrying Isabella Sarah Moorsom, whose father was a Captain in the Royal Navy and whose grandfather was Vice-Admiral Sir Robert Moorsom, KB, a gallant seaman who commanded HMS *Revenge* under Nelson at the Battle of

Trafalgar. By now the Laurences' Jewish past had completely disappeared and they became the quintessential English middle-class family.

The Reverend Percival and his wife Isabella had a number of children, and their eldest son, Henry Hamilton, born in 1864, became a barrister. After he married a solicitor's daughter, Mary Butler, in 1895, the couple emigrated to Guyana where Tim's father, Guy, was born the following year. Henry practised law for many years in Guyana before returning to England where he died in 1923 at the age of fifty-nine. His wife survived him by thirty years, dying in 1953 at the family home in Kent.

Tim's father married the former Barbara Symons, and the first of their two sons, Jonathan, was born in Tunbridge Wells in 1952. Tim followed in 1955, his birthplace being Camberwell in London.

*   *   *

The three years that Tim spent working at Buckingham Palace gave him an insight into the Royal Family circle that has proved invaluable since he himself became part of it. He escorted the Princess of Wales to fashionable restaurants such as San Lorenzo in Kensington, and he was photographed alongside the Duchess of York shortly after she married Prince Andrew. His tour of duty on board the Royal Yacht had taught him how to mix well with people from many walks of life, and although he had never enjoyed small-talk, he developed the necessary social skills that are integral to the life of a successful courtier. The Queen and Prince Philip both found him to be a congenial and efficient Aide, and the only hiatus in his upward path came when his affectionate letters to the Princess Royal were stolen.

The couple had managed to keep their relationship secret with the help of accommodating friends and Tim's neighbours in Winchester. The Princess would visit him frequently, often taking Peter and Zara with her. This went on for many months without anyone from the Press getting a notion of what was happening under their noses. Then out of the blue, as described in Chapter 5, a number of letters written by Tim to the Princess were stolen from her desk at Windsor Castle and offered to a newspaper. The editor declined to publish them (at first he thought it was a hoax) but once their authenticity had been established he handed them to the police.

At this time Tim was virtually unknown outside the Royal Household and he might have remained so if the Palace Press Office had not issued their statement naming him as the author of the letters. Tim thought this would mean the end of his career, both as a Royal servant and as a naval officer. He remembered what had happened to Peter Townsend, King George VI's Equerry, when it was discovered that he was in love with Princess Margaret: Townsend had been banished from Court and his RAF career in essence was finished at a stroke.

However, Tim was to be pleasantly surprised when the Queen, realizing how serious her daughter was about him, showed her support by including him in a number of engagements shortly after the revelation. The Duke of Edinburgh was not so welcoming, however. His initial reaction was icy fury that a trusted servant of the Queen had behaved in such a manner towards her still married daughter. Senior members of the Royal Household were equally horrified and Tim was given the cold shoulder by several of them for some weeks after the incident. The phrase 'Mad or bad' was muttered in the Palace corridors when Tim's name was mentioned. When it later became clear that he had survived the furore and might indeed even become a member of the Royal Family, those same courtiers were just as dismayed at the thought of possibly having to call him Sir in future.

The theft of the letters and their subsequent reappearance, plus the Palace statement confirming him as the author, all took their toll on Tim. In the weeks immediately following the incident he lost over a stone in weight and had to play hide-and-seek with the world's media. He was beginning to find out in startling fashion what being in the public eye can mean. He also learned to adopt the Royal Family's unofficial motto, 'Never complain, Never explain.' It was to stand him in good stead in the years to come.

Shortly afterwards his secondment to the Palace came to an end. It was not as a result of anything he had done or said, it was just that his three years were up and it was time for the next man to take over. Before he left the Queen showed how pleased she was with his performance as her Equerry by making him a Member of the Royal Victorian Order, her own personal Order of Chivalry.

Tim's naval career appeared to stagnate for a time when he was appointed military assistant to the Secretary of State for Defence shortly before he married. For two and a half years he was chained to a desk in Whitehall while acting as 'bag-carrier' for his minister. His office was just along the corridor from that of the Director of Public Relations for the Royal Navy who spent a little too much of his time answering questions about his famous colleague. Tim was said by his fellow officers to be 'friendly but careful'. He didn't make any new close friends and rarely joined his colleagues at office parties or private dinners. On the credit side, he also resisted all overtures by senior officers to cultivate a relationship.

In 1995 his well-known longing to return to sea duties was rewarded when he was promoted to the rank of Captain—adding a fourth stripe to his sleeve and with a pay rise of nearly £100 a week—and given command of HMS *Cumberland*. The *Cumberland* is a Type-22 frigate built at Yarrow in 1986 and said to possess the fire-power of a cruiser. When Captain Laurence took over, she had already seen active service in the Adriatic off Bosnia and her 250 officers and crew welcomed their new young skipper enthusiastically. In August 1996, Tim was given command of the flotilla guarding the Falkland Islands.

In the comparatively short time they have been married, the Princess Royal and her husband have been seen together at public functions more often than she and Mark Phillips were during the entire eighteen years of their married life. The Court Circular in *The Times* and *Daily Telegraph*, which lists the comings and goings of the Royal Family, frequently includes the words 'The Princess Royal, accompanied by Captain Timothy Laurence RN' when they record her activities. He appears at her side whenever he is in London and free from his naval duties and whenever Her Royal Highness attends a sporting occasion, such as one of Scotland's rugby matches (she is Patron of the Scottish Rugby Union). He loves the limelight but is clever enough not to try to steal it from his wife and is the perfect consort for a woman who has spent a lifetime in the public eye. He knows precisely where to stand and how to behave, and his years of training as a Royal Equerry have taught him how to converse brilliantly with anyone from a Prime Minister to the local road-sweeper. In a sense, he is now doing for nothing for the Princess the job he was paid to do for the Queen for three years.

In an effort to assert his own position as husband, Tim initially rented a flat in Dolphin Square, Pimlico, where he and the Princess stayed when they had to be in London during the working week. It was a very modest apartment with no servants' quarters. The only extra accommodation they had was a small room for their duty police officer's use. There was nothing to stop the couple using the Princess's suite of rooms on the second floor of Buckingham Palace which she has retained for over twenty years. It is roomy and spacious, with a dining-room, sitting-room and two bedrooms, but Tim Laurence wanted to show his independence, and so in the early months of the marriage he and his wife lived in Pimlico, an area the Princess Royal had probably only previously seen from the inside of a Royal limousine or looked down on from one of the helicopters of The Queen's Flight as it took off from the gardens of the Palace. By July 1995 the couple felt no further need of the flat, however, and they left Dolphin Square. Today they both use the Buckingham Palace suite when necessary, but at the time of writing, they are preparing to move into new accommodation being made ready for them in St James's Palace, where among their neighbours will be the Prince of Wales.

The Laurences appear to be an ideal couple. To an outsider theirs seems to be a perfect partnership and it is not unusual for Tim to tell his wife to calm down if he thinks she is going a bit over the top, even when others are present; something Mark Phillips would not have dreamt of doing. Mark was and is his own man, but where the Princess was concerned, he found it easier to let her have her own way—at least in public.

As a full-time officer in the Royal Navy Tim Laurence earns around £43,000 a year, hardly enough to keep the Queen's daughter in the style she is used to, but she has a substantial fortune of her own with the Trust Fund arranged by the Queen many years ago of which the Senior Trustee is one of Her Majesty's oldest friends, her racing manager, the Earl of Carnarvon. It was he who actually signed the purchase document when the Queen bought Gatcombe Park and he still oversees much of the Princess's financial affairs.

Tim has become a popular stepfather to the Princess's two children, Peter and Zara. Wisely, he has never tried to take their own father's place, even though, with the Princess now in her late forties, he and she are unlikely to have any children of their own. His relationship with Mark Phillips is civilized and amicable; they shoot together and meet at Gatcombe fairly often, and when they and the Princess meet, the three of them always seem remarkably relaxed in one another's company.

Someone who has had occasion to meet Tim under diferent circumstances over the years is Captain Norman Lloyd-Edwards, Lord Lieutenant of South Glamorgan, one of whose duties is to welcome members of the Royal Family to his part of South Wales. Captain Lloyd-Edwards is the perfect diplomat who has managed to remain on the friendliest of terms with both the Prince and Princess of Wales, in spite of their acrimonious marriage break-up.

He recalls the first time he met Tim Laurence. 'We were both guests at a dinner being held in Middle Temple. My host was Sir Tasker Watkins VC and Tim's was a retired Admiral. We hardly spoke during the function but found ourselves standing together on the pavement outside afterwards looking for a taxi. One came along and we decided to share. By this time he was already very much in the public eye because of his rumoured relationship with the Princess Royal, and indeed, it turned out to be only about a week before their engagement was announced. Anyway, we got into the taxi and the only thing I can remember was trying desperately to avoid mentioning the one thing I was dying to talk about—him and the Princess. He had obviously been schooled not to drop any hints and we spent the entire journey chatting about the Navy. He honed reticence to a fine art and when he spoke it was only in single sentences. He was always thinking about what he was going to say before he said it and there was nothing spontaneous about him. I've since met him a number of times on formal occasions, such as when he accompanied the Prince of Wales, Prince William and Prince Harry to Cardiff to see Wales play Scotland in the rugby international in February 1996. Tim was still quiet, taciturn to a degree, never giving anything away. One got the impression that he was totally reliable, rather "strong and silent" and yet with a determined streak in his make-up. As a naval officer myself I fully believe he will make "Flag" rank entirely on his own merits and through his own efforts. One thing that impressed me greatly about Tim on that Saturday afternoon was the way in which he and Prince William got on. They obviously liked each other very much and Prince William spent most of the afternoon chatting with Tim. There was an easy relationship between them that was very pleasant to see and if Tim seemed cautious with the rest of the party, he certainly was fully at ease with the young Prince.'

Tim Laurence has adapted brilliantly to life in the Royal Family. He mixes freely with his wife's old friends and has introduced her to several of his. Caroline Nunneley, one of the Princess's Ladies-in-Waiting, asked him to become godfather to her infant son, and he takes his role very seriously, as indeed he does with everything he undertakes. It wasn't simply a case of allowing his name to be used and just turning up at the christening; Tim made enquiries about his responsibilities to the child and is prepared to fulfil them to the best of his ability. Birthdays and other significant occasions will not be forgotten. That is not his way.

Andrew Parker Bowles says that the Princess Royal seems exactly the same to him as she has always been, but others have told him that she is much more relaxed since marrying Tim: 'They are a great team.'

Tim's ambition is to stay in the Royal Navy as long as he can, and he will not be hampered by the situation that hindered Mark Phillips's military career. Tim will be allowed to go wherever the Navy posts him; he would not have it any other way, and even though the Navy is making the same sort of cuts that the other branches of the Armed Forces are being forced to accept, he could end up as an Admiral if his progress continues as it has so far. That is his aim, and one in which he is fully supported by his wife—and also by the Queen. His Royal connections certainly will not do him any harm, but as the Services become more and more of a meritocracy, promotion to the topmost ranks becomes increasingly difficult. If an officer reaches the giddy heights these days it is because he deserves to be there and not because of the people he knows. One of Tim's brothers-in-law, the Duke of York, also had a successful naval career with a definite plus in his favour when he saw active service in the Falklands campaign as a helicopter pilot, acquitting himself well under fire. It is the sort of detail that looks attractive on an officer's CV, and being able to wear a medal earned in battle singles one out as being rather special. But the Duke has now indicated his wish to leave the Navy.

While Tim Laurence's tour of duty in Northern Ireland could not really be compared with action in the Falklands, he has none the less seen active service and so far has done nothing to blot his copybook or interrupt his climb to the top. His father-in-law rose to become an Admiral of the

Fleet, so who is to say that Tim could not do the same? If he does, it will not be because he is married to the daughter of his Commander-in-Chief, but because he has earned the position.

The price he has had to pay, and will continue to pay, for becoming a member of the Royal Family, is to learn to cope with the loneliness which membership of that little group involves. He can never relax totally in the company of strangers and never again will he be permitted the luxury of Wardroom gossip. Opinions which in the past would have been regarded as just that and nothing more, now take on an added significance when they come from the mouth of someone who is part of the Sovereign's (and Commander-in-Chief's) family. He realizes this and acts accordingly. What others might regard as arrogance and suspicion is in fact Tim's way of coping with the reality of his present unique situation.

CHAPTER EIGHT

GATCOMBE PARK

The house that the Princess Royal and Tim Laurence call home is just over 200 years old and stands in 1200 acres of superb country in the most beautiful part of Gloucestershire, known as the 'Royal triangle' from the fact that the Prince of Wales's house, Highgrove, is just a few miles to the south, with Prince and Princess Michael of Kent completing the trio of Royal homes at nearby Nether Lypiatt.

Gatcombe Park lies in a fold of the Cotswolds between the villages of Avening and Minchinhampton and was built in 1720 by Edward Sheppard, a wealthy sheep breeder and wool merchant who lived there with his family for many years. His son inherited the estate but sold it in 1814 to David Ricardo, a Member of Parliament and prominent political economist. It was Ricardo who made several important alterations to the house, employing the architect Basevi to turn it into the property it basically still is today.

The house changed hands a number of times during the next century before, in 1940, it came into the possession of the multi-millionaire textile manufacturer Samuel Courtauld. He was also the father-in-law of the late Lord (Rab) Butler, one of Britain's most prominent Members of Parliament in the fifties and sixties, who became a Cabinet Minister and was said to be 'the best Prime Minister Britain never had'. On retiring from politics, Lord Butler became Master of Trinity College, Cambridge, and when he heard that Princess Anne and her then husband, Mark Phillips, were looking for a country home, he suggested that they might care to consider his old family house, Gatcombe Park.

It was an inspired suggestion but one which the young couple needed even more inspiration to take seriously. When they first went to view it, Gatcombe had not been lived in fully for more than ten years. It was riddled with damp, there were no rooms fit for occupation, and the electric wiring was in such a dangerous condition that it had to be replaced throughout. The kitchen looked as if nothing had been done to it for fifty years, which

111

was probably the case, and the bathrooms were in a similarly dilapidated state. But the structure of the house was sound, the adjoining stable block was just what the Phillipses wanted to house their horses, and the view from the front of the house was, and remains, outstanding.

They fell for the house the moment they saw it, even though, as the Princess told me, 'It was far too big; it needed everything doing to it and we had not anticipated buying anything with quite so much land attached.' An arable farm of 500 acres went with the estate, which meant the couple had to rethink their plans. They had been looking for a place with just twenty or thirty acres in order to work their horses, but Gatcombe, with its large acreage, could not be run on a part-time basis. It needed someone to organize its management. However, this also solved another problem. Mark was going to leave the Army anyway to concentrate on his riding career, and the farm seemed the ideal way of combining two corresponding interests.

Another difficulty, of course, was that Mark did not have the money to pay for the house himself—at the time, as a Captain in 1st The Queen's Dragoon Guards, his salary was around £4,000 a year. The Princess's Trust Fund could have been used if necessary, but the problem of financing the deal was solved by the Queen agreeing to buy the property. The original asking price was some £700,000 but the property probably finally changed hands for slightly less than £500,000. It was an astute investment as today Gatcombe Park is worth in excess of £3 million.

Even though the newspapers of the day all reported that the Queen had given the house to the couple as a present, it was in fact given to the Princess alone. She is the owner and mistress of Gatcombe and, like Tim Laurence today, Mark had no financial holding in the estate at all (apart from a small mortgage he took out to fund some of the work that needed to be done). This is why the house did not figure in the divorce settlement when the Princess and Mark split up.

Of course the purchase of the house attracted its fair share of criticism, mainly from left-wing politicians, with the most public statement from a leading figure coming from Neil Kinnock (before he became Leader of the Labour Party). He said, 'I don't know which is worse—the Queen for being wealthy enough to give it to them, or them [sic] for having the neck to take it.'

Countless thousands of people have now seen the view that the Princess enjoyed on that first day, as they sample the delights of the Park when Gatcombe opens its doors to the public for its annual Horse Trials. But in the 1970s it was very easy to miss Gatcombe completely if you didn't know it was there. You cannot see it from the road and there is a long drive overhung with laurel bushes that stretches from the gateway that guards the main entrance to the estate. Gatcombe is located about one mile to the east of the village of Minchinhampton and there is no sign indicating the name of the house or, more particularly, of who lives there.

A small lodge is situated just inside the gates on the right-hand side and as you drive towards the house you see a security post, manned twenty-four hours a day by police from the Gloucestershire force, which has been so skilfully designed that it blends perfectly with the surrounding woodland. Just before you reach the house itself there is a divide in the drive. Visitors are directed to take the right fork, around the back of the house; the Princess and her family use the left fork, which leads directly to the front where they park their cars on the gravelled terrace.

Most people are quite surprised at their first sighting of Gatcombe, because it is not nearly so large as it looks in photographs. This illusion is created by the conservatory, added in 1829, which is attached to the house on the left side as you view it from the front. Without it, Gatcombe would appear as an elegant but comparatively modest country mansion.

The number of rooms totals thirty-two, including, as Mark Phillips once admitted, 'every lavatory and large cupboard'. Inside, the house is surprisingly compact and cosy. The hall is flagstoned and full of riding boots, wellingtons and walking sticks, with copies of *Country Life* and *The Field* lying on the long table down one side of the hall. There is also a water bowl which is kept filled for whichever of the dogs needs it after coming indoors. Legend has it that the ghost of a large, headless black dog has roamed the grounds around the mansion for generations but neither the Princess nor any member of her family has yet admitted to seeing it.

The drawing-room opens off the hall to the left as you enter and you pass through it to get to the sitting-room. The drawing-room has an open fireplace in which logs from the estate are burnt. And one thing that becomes apparent to a visitor in winter is that even though the Princess Royal never forgets who she is for a moment, she has none of the old-style arrogance that still attaches to certain members of the Royal Family. For example, she wouldn't dream of calling a servant to put logs on the fire; she picks them up and does it herself, without a moment's thought or hesitation, unlike her late Great-uncle Henry, the Duke of Gloucester, who once sat and watched a coal smouldering on the carpet for several minutes while he waited for a footman to come and remove it.

The drawing-room, with its deep armchairs and sofas, is the most comfortable room in the house, and the only hint one gets of the identity of the owner of the house is the number of silver-framed photographs of Royalty, past and present, adorning the coffee tables. It is in this room that the Princess receives visitors—one example of her thoughtfulness is that if an officer from one of the nearby Service bases with which she is associated has to make a courtesy call, she will invite him to Gatcombe, to save the inconvenience of having to travel all the way up to Buckingham Palace.

Leading off the drawing-room is the sitting-room which doubles as the Princess's office. The desk where she works on her papers for several hours every day when she is at Gatcombe was a wedding present from the Duke of Edinburgh, and is placed in a beautiful box window, but deliberately sideways on so that the Princess is not distracted by the splendid views across the park.

Anne and Tim frequently have their lunch in this room, served to them on trays as they sit side by side on the sofa in front of the fireplace. The dining-room, which is reserved for more formal occasions and can seat a dozen people in comfort, lies on the opposite side of the hall from the drawing-room. Sideboards are covered with the Princess's collection of Georgian silver, a gift from the Queen, which is brought out when she and Tim give a dinner party, and when the table is fully set it glitters with sparkling crystal, polished silver, beautiful china and elegant Irish linen. Gatcombe may be the most unceremonious of Royal homes, but a formal dinner party is a special occasion; nobody does it better than the Princess. She is a perfectly organized hostess, relaxed and with the happy knack of being able to put her guests at their ease as soon as they enter the room.

Beyond the dining-room is a smaller room which used to be Mark's study and was usually filled to overflowing with books and video-tapes of the television programmes neither he nor the Princess had had the time to watch. The books you find at Gatcombe do not include many of the classics but there is a fine set of first editions by the most successful of thriller writers with a horsey background, Dick Francis. He is the Princess's favourite author, and of course he also has another Royal connection in that he was the Queen Mother's steeplechase jockey for many years.

When Princess Anne was first setting up home at Gatcombe she was offered a selection of some of the finest paintings in the Royal Collection. She politely refused them all, preferring sets of prints with a sporting theme. When she was married to Mark nearly all the pictures in the house showed various aspects of equestrian life. After the divorce he took many of his pictures with him to his new house and there was a general re-hanging of paintings which now reflect a more catholic taste. There has been a subtle change in the personality of Gatcombe since Tim Laurence's arrival and there is nothing remotely imitative about the house today.

The kitchen at Gatcombe is on the ground floor and was one of the rooms that needed to be completely revamped when the Princess took over the house in 1976. It has all the conveniences and appliances one would expect to find in any modern home but it still retains the old-style country house look. Also on the ground floor is the sitting-room for the police officers who guard the Princess, containing armchairs, tables and a television set. A spare bedroom for the duty officer leads off this sitting-room. When Peter and Zara were younger and attended local schools, one of the police officers would often drive them to and fro if the Princess was not available, but these days, with both children away at boarding school, they do not have to act as baby-sitters.

An impressive staircase leads to the first floor where the eight bedrooms are located. This is the area where the most dramatic alterations took place when the Princess became the owner of Gatcombe. Until then the bathrooms were mainly at the front of the house, overlooking the park, with the bedrooms at the back with no views at all and very little sun, as the house is built into the side of a rock face, without space for even a small rear garden.

All this was reversed, and today the main bedroom suite has a fantastic view over the valley below, with a stone-built folly, perhaps more accurately described as an unusual pyramid tower, in the distance. Upstairs the house is light and airy. The top floor has a huge attic space where in the old days the servants all had their cramped quarters. This was converted into a nursery wing with its own bedrooms, bathrooms, kitchen and playroom. When the children were young enough to need a nanny, she lived here too. But Gatcombe has never been the sort of house where children were restricted to the upper quarters. The entire house has always had a lived-in look and there was always plenty of evidence of children about the place. Even today, when the family is all together, there is a delightful feeling that nowhere is sacrosanct. Gatcombe is without doubt the most informal and comfortable of all the Royal residences, and the lady of the house has stamped her personality on it from the moment she moved in.

There is a very small domestic staff to look after the house and it is the only Royal residence not to have a butler. There used to be one but these days the Princess sees no need, so she makes do with just a cook/house-keeper and one local woman who helps with the general cleaning and dusting. There are no legions of servants running back and forth as one might expect in a Royal household, and when you realize that there are over eighty staff in Clarence House alone, it is not difficult to see why the Princess Royal is reputed to be the most practical member of her famous family.

The Gatcombe estate grows winter barley, and has both beef and dairy cattle, but it is not self-supporting as an agricultural enterprise and is run by just four people: a working manager and three full-time staff, a tractor driver, a stockman and a woodman. At harvest-time the children and their parents all lend a hand, and extra student labour is recruited from the nearby Royal Agricultural College at Cirencester. Nearly a quarter of Gatcombe Park is covered by woodlands but a gamekeeper is not employed and no one would describe Gatcombe as a sporting estate. Nevertheless, the Princess loves to organize shooting parties at which friends such as Jackie Stewart—who is of near Olympic standard as a shot—enjoy a fine day's sport.

In fact it is the shooting that causes the only mildly serious disagreements between the Princess and her former husband. Mark needs the estate to make money, and as a day's shooting can be very profitable he wants as many days as he can get. But on those days when the Princess invites friends to shoot, no money changes hands, of course. So when there is a dispute over which of them will have the shooting on a particular day, the discussions can become rather heated. It is often Tim Laurence who smooths things over. He acts as mediator and settles matters without appearing to favour either side. Both Anne and Mark have reason to be grateful for his diplomatic skills.

At one time the park was practically overrun with foxes, but no hunting takes place for security reasons, and the only time the estate is open to the public is when the annual Horse Trials take place in August. This was a commercial enterprise started by the Princess and Mark Phillips in 1983 because, as Mark said at the time, 'Princess Anne and I have had a lot out of the sport and we would like to put something back.' It was an immediate success and has grown in size and stature until it is now regarded as one of the most important dates in the equestrian calendar.

Apart from opening the park to the public several days a year, the Princess takes little part in local life. When the children were small and attended the village school, she would drive them to and from their lessons if she was at home, and she was friendly towards the other mothers she met. But with her commitments elsewhere she does not really have the time to mix socially in the life of Minchinhampton, nor is she a regular churchgoer at home, although she always attends Morning Service with her mother when she is at Windsor, Sandringham or Balmoral.

When the Princess first moved into Gatcombe in 1976, the estate was just 733 acres. A year later an opportunity arose to enlarge it considerably but with it came certain financial problems. Mark Phillips wanted to buy a few extra fields belonging to the adjoining Aston Farm. However, when he approached the elderly owner, Captain Vaisey Davis, he was offered the entire farm of 530 acres. He and the Princess knew that the offer was too good to turn down: it clearly made good economic sense to join the two properties together, but they did not have the money to buy it outright. They began negotiations with a financial organization to fund them on a 'lease-back' basis.

One evening they were dining with the Queen and told her what they proposed to do. Her Majesty was not too keen on their becoming involved with an outside company and offered to finance them, saying, 'Why can't I be the institution? I'll buy it and rent it to you in the same way.' So in November 1977 the Queen bought

Aston Farm and became Mark Phillips's landlord, which she still is as he moved into the farmhouse when he became divorced from the Princess Royal. It is an arrangement that suits all parties as Mark still runs the farm and is nearby when the children are at home, so they can see him whenever they wish. There are no problems about formal visiting rights and so on; the children come and go as they please between both parents. They have the best of both worlds.

The total acreage of the two farms is now an impressive 1,263 acres, and Gatcombe is at once the most informal of Royal residences and also far and away the most comfortable. The Princess Royal has turned a cold, damp and austere house into a warm, welcoming home which she and her family love and to which the rest of the Royal Family are all pleased to be invited. The Queen visits occasionally but she has never stayed overnight; the house is not really suitable to accommodate her and the staff who would need to accompany her. The Princess realizes this and accepts the difficulties, unlike her brother, Prince Charles, who is said to be unhappy that his mother has never once been an overnight guest at Highgrove.

CHAPTER NINE

FRIENDS AND NEIGHBOURS

The Princess Royal has either been very lucky or brilliantly selective in her choice of friends, for not one has ever broken the strict code of silence that binds them. It's not that she imposes any rules on her close circle, they simply know that if they start talking to the media about what goes on when they visit Gatcombe or when she and Tim visit them, the doors will close with chilling finality. They don't live under a threat, they actually like to keep their privacy almost as much as she does.

As with most people who share common interests, the Princess's closest friends nearly all come from the horsey set. The man for whom she rides out, David 'Duke' Nicholson and his wife Dinah, have long been confidants and special friends who enjoy her hospitality at Gatcombe. In turn the Princess Royal loves to sit at the kitchen table at the Nicholsons' house and drink a mug of coffee while listening to the latest gossip from the racecourse.

Jane and Timothy Holderness-Roddam have been included in the group for many years. They live a short drive from Gatcombe in a remote hamlet just the other side of the M4 motorway. Both spend most of their off-duty hours on horseback, and as a former Olympic rider, Jane has a special affinity with, and understanding of, the Princess's ways. This, of course, was one of the reasons why she was asked to become a Lady-in-Waiting in the first place, and when she is a guest at Gatcombe there is no mistress/servant atmosphere: she is as welcome as any friend from any walk of life. The Princess Royal has the happy knack of being able to separate her private life from her professional life.

Caroline Nunneley, another Lady-in-Waiting, first got to know the Princess through her previous job working for Alison Oliver, the Princess's riding coach, and later through her ex-husband, Malcolm Wallace, who was Director-General of the British Equestrian Federation. She has retained the friendship of her employer through a divorce and remarriage, and also manages to balance being a close friend with her duties as a Royal Aide.

Peter Gibbs, the Princess's Private Secretary and most senior staff member, has also been invited to shooting parties at Gatcombe, where his boss treats him exactly as she does any other guest. On these occasions there is no shop talk and Peter is received with as much ceremony—or lack of it—as anyone else.

Alison Oliver and her husband are another couple who go back a long way with the Princess Royal. It was Alison whom Anne telephoned on the night of the kidnap attempt in 1974, immediately after she had spoken to her family. Alison heard of the incident on the car radio as she was driving home and when she arrived at her Oxfordshire farmhouse the telephone was ringing. It was Anne, saying, 'I'm all right. I didn't want you to worry.' Alison said later it was the best phone call she had ever had: 'It was typically thoughtful of her to think of me at such a moment. She knew I would be worried sick.'

The Olivers have been among Anne's closest friends since, at eighteen, the Princess first went to Alison Oliver for coaching in riding. They have shared the triumphs and disasters that any sportsman encounters, and Anne is gracious enough to admit that much of the success she achieved as an international rider was due to Alison Oliver. Alison is also the only person, outside her own family, who has ever been allowed to call the Princess by her Christian name—this when she was still a teenager. They had started to train together and Alison felt it would be cumbersome to have to call her new pupil 'Your Royal Highness' all the time. The Princess resolved the problem by inviting Alison to call her Anne. Her actual words were, 'Call me Anne, it's the simplest way.'

Because the Princess Royal spends most of her working week operating from her office in Buckingham Palace, and her husband is often away at sea, social life at Gatcombe is fairly restricted. Guests are still invited for a day's shooting in the season and the odd dinner party and weekend house party are held when the couple can find a mutually convenient date in their diaries. But compared with other members of the Royal Family—Princess Margaret is an inveterate party-giver, and the Queen Mother enjoys few things more than having friends for lunch or dinner several times a week—the Laurences are practically hermits.

Entertainment at Gatcombe is a combination of the informal and the conventional. When guests are invited for the weekend they are told, 'Just bring a pair of jeans and a black tie.' This lets them know that the daylight hours will be spent relaxing around the house or tramping through the grounds, while Saturday evening dinner is an occasion when one is expected to dress up a little.

The Princess Royal is a born organizer, and as she hates not to have every moment of her own life filled, she also feels that her guests must not be allowed to lounge around doing nothing. She marshals them into long walks over Gatcombe's

1,200 acres, often finding them little jobs to do around the estate as well. Couch potatoes are not welcome. As most of her guests are people she has known for years, she is well aware of what they like to do, and in turn, they know what to expect. She takes a personal interest in their comfort and will inspect every guest bedroom to make sure that they have everything they could need. She chooses bedside books which she thinks they will enjoy, ensures that fresh flowers are placed in the rooms, and checks the bathrooms herself. It's not that she doesn't trust her staff; it's just that, as a perfectionist, she has to satisfy herself that everything is as it should be. This is a trait she has inherited from her mother, who still inspects every room when guests are staying at one of her homes, whether it is a full State Visit to Buckingham Palace, or a private weekend at Sandringham.

Once the Princess's guests have bathed and changed for the evening, they meet downstairs in the drawing-room for drinks. Anything one could ask for is available and neither the Princess nor Tim has any objection to their guests getting slightly merry. She drinks no alcohol at all, but Tim enjoys a glass or two of good wine.

After half an hour or so, dinner is served across the hall in the elegant dining-room. The Princess sits at one end of the table, beautifully laid with her collection of Georgian silver, with Tim at the other, and the food is handed through a serving hatch from the kitchen next door, so that it is always hot (which has not always been the case in Royal residences).

The Princess Royal has simple tastes in food. She enjoys good, wholesome meals, perfectly prepared and cooked, but usually without any exotic sauces. The fare could not be described as sophisticated; on the other hand it could not be faulted in any way either. The Princess Royal has only one standard, and it applies equally to everything she does or is associated with—perfection. No one has ever come away from her table feeling hungry, or dissatisfied with what he or she has been offered, although one regular at Gatcombe, who asked not to be named as he wants to remain on the guest list, said, 'She does occasionally get things slightly wrong, such as serving Liebfraumilch with pheasant.'

Dinner-table conversation is always lively, with no one deferring to their hostess. She enjoys a vigorous argument, even if she isn't too keen on losing one. They may concentrate on horses for part of the time, but never exclusively. The topics range from sex to movies, music and money, with only one topic excluded. That is the Royal Family itself. There is an unwritten rule that the Princess Royal's relations are never discussed, though how it has been possible in recent years to go through an entire evening without once mentioning the love life of the Prince of Wales or the finances of the Duchess of York, strains the imagination a little. If by chance some reference is made to a member of the Royal Family, guests and hostess will invariably use his or her full title. There is no such informality as referring to the Queen as 'your mother' or 'my mother', or the Prince of Wales as Charles. He finds even Princes Charles too familiar for his taste, insisting on the Prince of Wales at all times. The only members of the family who use Christian names and other endearments in front of outsiders are the Duke and Duchess of York. For example, when the Duchess is talking to one of her show-business friends, Billy Connolly perhaps, she would talk about 'Andrew' and not 'His Royal Highness' or 'The Duke'.

If all this sounds as though entertainment at Gatcombe is stilted and uneasy, the complete opposite is true. Everyone is relaxed and informal, with the Princess being particularly concerned if a guest is there for the first time. Surprisingly to some people, the Princess Royal quite likes the idea of friends dropping in unexpectedly, explaining, 'It's easier for them to know when I'm here than the other way around. They know they are welcome, and I like people to ring up or simply to drop in if they are in the vicinity.' It's a degree of informality that is at odds with the image most outsiders have of her. Nevertheless, to all her friends, even those who have known her more than twenty years, she remains Your Royal Highness or Ma'am. (One of the most difficult decisions Tim Laurence had to make was picking exactly the right moment to call his future wife Anne, after years of having to bow his head whenever they met and addressing her as 'Your Royal Highness'.) Nobody has instructed the Princess's friends in the protocol, there is nothing written down, although the Palace will give guidelines if asked. It is just that all Anne's friends, male and female, know that it is the right way to address her, and both they, and she, feel more comfortable with it.

The Princess Royal is arguably the most Royal of all Princesses, with blue blood flowing in her veins from both parents. Yet even her aunt, Princess Margaret, who has been described as the 'most regal of Princesses' (and there are many who would testify that her behaviour on occasions bears this out), has to admit that her mother, while becoming a Queen Consort on marriage, was actually born a commoner.

The Princess Royal could so easily have become a conventional Sovereign's daughter, mixing only with suitable young people chosen by her parents and carrying out public duties where there was no danger of her getting her hands dirty. But her lifestyle, while comfortable in the extreme at home, with all the advantages that money and position can secure, is otherwise more normal than many people would expect of the Queen's only daughter.

Brigadier Andrew Parker Bowles is without doubt one of the closest of the Princess Royal's friends. They have known each other for nearly thirty years, and even though they first met when Andrew was playing polo at Windsor, he is the first to admit that nothing in his background could justify a claim that he came from the horsey set. In fact, in spite of his aristocratic pedigree (his family, the de Traffords, own most of Manchester and have some of the city's most famous landmarks, Trafford Park and the Old Trafford football and cricket grounds, named after them), he did not learn to ride until he joined the Army, became a cavalry officer, and eventually rose to become Commanding Officer of the Household Cavalry (and Silver Stick-in-Waiting to the Queen). His success as a rider culminated in his becoming one of the few amateur jockeys not only to ride in but to complete the toughest race in the world, the Grand National, in spite of the fact that he had broken his back in an earlier racing accident.

But it wasn't a mutual interest in horses that first drew Andrew and Anne together, it was a purely physical attraction of two young people who rather fancied each other. Their relationship settled down to a lasting friendship, and he is godfather to Zara Phillips and a financial Trustee of both Peter and Zara.

Andrew Parker Bowles, a large, amiable man, spent thirty-five years in the Army and now lives in a tiny hamlet in Wiltshire. His present home is a charming house of great comfort where one is left in no doubt of the owner's former profession. Military photographs and paintings line the walls, a flag is draped over the filing cabinet in his office, which leads directly off the sitting-room, and his cavalry officer's sabre faces you when you enter the hall. Pride of place is given to his favourite picture, a signed photograph of himself being congratulated by his admitted heroine Queen Elizabeth, the Queen Mother, after winning the Grand Military Gold Cup in 1974.

Andrew has retained the friendship of Mark Phillips as well as of the Princess Royal since their divorce, and the unwelcome publicity which surrounded the break-up of his own first marriage has done nothing to change his relationship with the Princess. In fact he is probably the closest friend she has today, and Tim Laurence, a relative newcomer to the Royal circle, has also been successfully included in the relationship. Andrew and Tim get on brilliantly and their wives also get on well. Andrew and Rosemary visit Gatcombe occasionally when Tim has leave and in turn he and the Princess enjoy quiet dinners at the Parker Bowleses' house, just over a quarter of an hour's drive away.

Andrew says that one of the ways in which Tim has influenced his wife is by instilling in her his enthusiasm for gardening. 'Mark was never in the least bit interested in gardening and neither, really, was the Princess Royal. She has always been fairly knowledgeable about trees, which was an interest she inherited from the Duke of Edinburgh, but flowers and plants were not her thing. All that has changed. Tim is an ardent gardener (his father was an expert), and these days you will often see them both at Gatcombe getting their hands dirty or delving through gardening catalogues. I've given them a few plants from time to time and when I've been over to Gatcombe I've noticed that they seem to be thriving.'

Andrew also believes that he has never seen the Princess happier than she is at present. 'Tim has obviously been good for her. He is not the sort of man she can dominate, even if she wanted to. He is definitely his own man, highly intelligent, with exactly the right temperament for handling her. Mark was and is a delightful person, but in terms of personality the Princess left him standing. Where he was indecisive over the smallest issues, she would make up her mind instantly. She has always known what she wants and as a result she is not always the most patient of women with anyone who dithers.'

Apart from their close personal relationship, Andrew Parker Bowles and the Princess Royal share a professional interest in several organizations. They are both involved in the International League for the Protection of Horses, and the Worshipful Company of Farriers, whose motto is 'No foot, no horse'. The Princess became Master of the Farriers Company in 1984—the first woman to do so—and Andrew Parker Bowles says that one of her first acts was to help solve a delicate problem involving a wealthy and influential overseas owner, who was using a non-registered and untrained farrier to shoe his horses. The Princess Royal spoke directly to the man concerned and the matter was sorted out immediately. It was a case of everyone knowing what the problem was but being unable or unwilling to risk the anger of a powerful owner. The Princess, in her unique position, did not suffer such anxiety and went straight to the top.

With regard to her involvement in the other organizations, Andrew Parker Bowles says, 'She has been responsible for turning the Animal Health Trust into the number one Horse Veterinary organization in the world, and ninety per cent of the money the Trust now has was raised by her. She has arguably the best contacts among businessmen in industry and commerce anywhere in the country and she uses them for the benefit of the Trust. Nobody can turn her down and she really is a hands-on Patron or President or whatever other office she holds. She is never just another Royal name on a letter-head; she insists on taking an active role, attending committee meetings and then following up any decisions that have been taken to see that they have been acted upon.' And when it comes to using her Royal connections, apparently the Princess is not backward either. According to Andrew Parker Bowles, 'She hosts fund-raising parties on board the Royal Yacht *Britannia*, knowing that few people will refuse an invitation, and then she prises their cheque-books out of them. All in the cause of the charity.'

Malcolm Wallace is another of the Princess's oldest friends who, like Andrew Parker Bowles, was asked to become one of the three Trustees to Peter and Zara Phillips, a position he still holds today. In turn the Princess Royal is godmother to Wallace's elder son, Harry, a responsibility she takes tremendously seriously. 'She is a wonderful godmother and never forgets an anniversary, birthday or Christmas and she takes a great interest in all he's doing and his well-being. Both my children go to Gatcombe regularly, but these days our paths, the Princess's and mine, simply do not cross. We meet occasionally at the races when we have a natter and a joke but circumstances have caused us not to meet as often as we once did.'

Tall and spare of frame, Malcolm Wallace still looks every inch the Royal Horse Artillery Major he once was as Commanding Officer of The King's Troop. Arguably the most gregarious of her circle—the Princess has herself described him as 'the best raconteur in the business'—Malcolm is the one person who has seldom felt it necessary to bite his tongue when talking to the Princess Royal. He is now an executive with the Jockey Club, but in the days when he was Director-General of the British Equestrian Federation, he came into frequent contact, both socially and professionally, with the Princess. She was President of the Fédération Equestre Internationale (FEI) and their paths often crossed on business matters.

He recalled some of their more celebrated confrontations. 'We didn't always see eye to eye and it came to a head at one meeting we had in

Tokyo. I think she had probably had a bad morning and I came up with three proposals that I had been set by the Federation. She didn't agree with any of them and we had a real set-to, quite openly across the room. Later my Chairman told me I had overdone it a bit and upset Her Royal Highness. I replied that the Federation had paid £5,000 to send us to Tokyo and I wasn't going to waste their money by not saying anything. I added that I could guarantee that at that evening's cocktail party, as soon as she entered the room she would look for me, come across and say she hoped I hadn't minded the way things had gone that morning. I could have written the script as that was exactly the way it happened. She never sulked, and once an argument was over it was forgotten so far as she was concerned.' There are not too many people who would care to put their case as bluntly as Malcolm Wallace, but he knew the Princess better than most and also knew just how far he could go.

Their friendship goes back many years; he even rode for her for a season and says, 'She was the best owner I ever rode for. One day she drove, heavily pregnant with Peter, in a heatwave, from Sandhurst to Preston to watch me ride two of her horses. I turned one over in the show-jumping and the other over on the cross-country course. All she said was, "That's horses," shared her lunch with me and drove four horses home!'

Through his friendship with the Princess Malcolm became a frequent visitor to several of the Royal residences. 'I shot regularly at Sandringham for seventeen years as her guest and she was magnificent. Later, when she moved to Gatcombe and I went there, she was not quite so easygoing. I think the difference was that at Sandringham everything was taken care of by the Royal Household, so all she had to do was be there, while at Gatcombe, it was all her responsibility. She looked after everything personally and I think it did not come easily. This is not to say she was not a generous hostess, because she was, but one got the impression that the responsibility of organizing a whole day's shooting or a dinner party for eight or ten was a chore she could well do without. An important part of being a successful host or hostess is being able and happy to deal with trivia. The Princess has never been one for trivia. She leads a busy life and has little time for things of no importance, so this aspect of entertaining held no appeal for her. I felt that she was never too unhappy when the time came for everyone to go home.'

When Malcolm married his first wife, Caroline, they were both assimilated into the Princess Royal's social group, but since their divorce it is Caroline and her present husband who have remained, while Malcolm's friendship with Mark Phillips has strengthened—Mark is an old friend of Jane, Malcolm's wife. As Malcolm Wallace put it, 'It was inevitable, I suppose, that our positions would polarize. You cannot really have a divorced couple sitting at the same table with their new spouses alongside. Civilized behaviour goes only so far.'

Malcolm Wallace does not like to go into any details about the break-up of his first marriage, but he does remember with perfect clarity the events of one of the worst days in his life, and the reaction of his old friend the Princess Royal. 'When my wife left me and drove out of the house with the children—obviously not the happiest day of my life—the first person to phone me was Princess Anne. I was sitting in the kitchen, wondering what the hell to do, when she rang and spoke to me for an hour and a quarter. It was the nicest thing that anyone could have done at that time. I was very appreciative then and I still am. It was the action of a true friend. Shortly afterwards she asked me to go and stay at Gatcombe and, without interfering in any way, she let me unwind. She was there if I needed her. That's her style.'

Malcolm Wallace says that even though he rarely sees the Princess now he still regards her as a friend and he believes she thinks of him in the same way. However, even when he saw her on a regular basis he was always aware of her position. 'Having known her for so many years and been quite a close friend, I suppose it was odd that never once did she invite me, or others like me, to drop the Ma'am in private. As a serving officer I was sometimes spoken to by Generals and others far senior to me in rank who said that privately I should use their Christian names, knowing that on parade I didn't have to be reminded that it was Sir all the time. But throughout all the years I was a close friend and regular guest, at Gatcombe and Buckingham Palace, I always gave a neck-bow whenever we met and never addressed her as anything other than Ma'am or Your Royal Highness; mind you, nor did anyone else to my knowledge. But when you realize that the Prince of Wales, even as a child, had been taught to shake hands with his mother, the Queen, on the platform at Victoria Station, and not kiss her as most children would find it natural to do, it's understandable that to someone like the Princess Royal, formal behaviour is second nature also.'

Also to be found around the dining table at Gatcombe is a selection of artists, sporting journalists (but no Royal rat-pack reporters), former racing drivers, actors, businessmen and the odd clergyman. It's an eclectic bunch but with one factor in common—they are all totally loyal to the Princess. She is the only member of the Royal Family not to have been betrayed by someone who has accepted her hospitality. Every other member of her family has suffered the indignity of hearing their private thoughts and dinner-table conversations repeated to the media. Not so the Princess Royal. The circle remains as tightly knit—and close-mouthed—today as it was twenty-five years ago.

Perhaps the most unusual of her friendships, in terms of the disparity of their respective backgrounds, is the one she shares with Jackie Stewart. It began a quarter of a century ago when they were both at the pinnacle of their particular sports and had been chosen as Sports Personalities of 1971. Stewart, who was raised in Scotland, the son of a garage owner, readily admits that he did not have much of an education. The reason for this was that he is slightly dyslexic, which in the days when he was at school was usually interpreted as being backward. This has since been disproved over and over again by the man who has risen to multimillionaire status by his own efforts as an international businessman. He was the most successful Formula One racing driver Britain ever produced, winning twenty-nine Grand Prix races, a record which still stands. Today he travels the world on behalf of his many commercial interests and has very nearly as high a profile as he did in his racing days.

He and the Princess hit it off from the moment they first met, and their friendship has never cooled. Stewart knew no members of the Royal Family back in the seventies, but he quickly became accepted by all of them and these days is as much at home with Prince Edward or the Duke of York as he ever was with his own mechanics.

Stewart has always been a confident, some might say slightly arrogant person. But he has never tried to be anything other than what he is and that is the secret of his success socially. The Princess Royal didn't care—even if she knew—what his background was, and accepted him for what he is. She admires excellence in others, be they a plumber or politician, and no one could ever deny that Jackie Stewart was anything other than the very best at his craft. It was a meeting of kindred spirits.

The Princess and her family have spent many happy holidays at the Stewarts' home in Switzerland, and Jackie and his wife Helen have been welcome guests at Gatcombe more times than any other couple. When Helen Stewart was invited to become godmother to Zara in 1981, she described her reaction as 'a delightful surprise and an honour'.

The age group of the Princess Royal's friends ranges from her contemporaries to men and women in their seventies. Although there are not too many of the latter, the former Dean of Windsor, the Rt Rev'd Michael Mann, comes into this category, as does Marmaduke 'Duke' Hussey, whose wife Lady Susan has known the Princess since she was a young girl.

Tim has been included as a matter of course and one of his strengths is that he is able to adapt to whatever circle he finds himself in. So even though his interests were not originally equestrian, he has managed to learn enough about horses to hold an intelligent conversation, and he is wise enough not to force his opinions on those he knows are more knowledgeable than he, though he is probably better educated than the majority of those who visit Gatcombe. He is popular with the Princess's friends and enjoys giving dinner parties and acting as host. His years as an Equerry have taught him how to handle himself in almost any situation and he is adept at avoiding embarrassing silences. As a partner to the Princess, Tim is definitely a social asset, though not too many of his naval colleagues are guests at Gatcombe.

The Princess Royal is close to her own family even if their paths do not cross as frequently as she would like. There is a curious formality about relationships within the Royal Family which is difficult for an outsider to understand.

For example, even though the Princess has a suite of rooms at Buckingham Palace and spends at least a couple of nights there most weeks, she has often gone for weeks without seeing her mother or father. The Queen's private apartments are on the first floor of the Palace overlooking Green Park. The Princess Royal's rooms are on the second floor facing up The Mall, less than two minutes' walk along the corridor and down the stairs. Yet she would never dream of simply walking into her mother's sitting-room without an invitation or, if she wanted to see the Queen, without ringing the Royal Page first to see if it was convenient. If the Queen knows that her daughter is in the Palace she might invite her to join her for tea, but even that is done through several intermediaries, never directly from mother to daughter.

There was one occasion when I was at Gatcombe and the butler (she had one in those days) came into the drawing-room to tell the Princess that the Queen was on the telephone (they do actually speak frequently on the phone). When the call was put through to her the Princess automatically stood up as she spoke to her mother, 150 miles away. I don't think she was even aware of this; it certainly wasn't done to impress me—but it did! It was just another example of the perfect manners she shows whenever her family is involved.

Life is a little more relaxed with her father, the Duke of Edinburgh, with whom she enjoys a relationship that is totally unqualified. Neither father nor daughter can see any wrong in the other and one way to really annoy either one is to criticize the other. If the Princess wants to talk to her father when they are both at Buckingham Palace she will use her direct line to him and he will occasionally pop his head around her door if he is passing. They are on exactly the same wavelength and there is an almost uncanny telepathy between them. She will sometimes let him see the draft of a speech she intends to deliver, for his comments, and she invariably knows in advance what passages he will give his views on. They also argue hammer and tongs about various topics in which they both have an interest, such as wildlife or conservation, but they always end up on the best of terms. It is one of the truly genuine father/daughter relationships and one that is cherished equally by both of them.

Friendship with a member of the Royal Family cannot be judged in the same terms one would apply to people who are not Royal. While the Queen and Prince Philip enjoy extremely close relationships with one or two men and women they have known for most of their lives, such as Countess Mountbatten of Burma and her husband, the film producer Lord Brabourne, and Lady Pamela Hicks and her designer husband David, the friendship extends only so far. It is impossible for outsiders to comprehend fully just how tightly knit the Royal Family are and how difficult it is to break in. Some people fool themselves for a while, believing they are part of the inner circle. What they do not initially realize is that there is a 'them and us' situation which can never be breached. No matter how high in status, wealth or social standing a person might be, if they are not Royal there is a line over which they cannot cross.

The same rules apply to them all, including the Princess Royal. She may honestly believe that her closest friends are the people she sees at home socially or those whom she and Tim may visit regularly. But a relationship with a non-Royal person can go only so far. The Royal Family find it hard enough to discuss intimate details of personal problems even among themselves; they would find it impossible—and unthinkable—to involve anyone outside the family. The Princess Royal has no one outside her own family with whom she would be willing, or feel able, to discuss, say, the marital difficulties of her brothers. And when she and Mark were going through their own problems, none of her closest companions, male or female, was even considered as someone she could confide in.

Hers is a solitary life in many ways. She has a wide circle of acquaintances, a few men and women she calls true friends, but when it comes to needing someone in whom she can trust without qualification, she has to turn inwards. Only someone who is Royal can really understand another Royal, and the exclusion extends to both the men she has married, so when it comes to real friendship, it is to her own family that the Princess looks. Her relationship with her father has never faltered, and that with her mother is closer now than it has ever been. They see each other more often since the Princess has been married to Tim than before. No one knows the reason, but whereas, in years gone by, the Princess would go for weeks without seeing the Queen, even when both were only yards from each other at Buckingham Palace, now they see each other frequently, and rarely do more than a couple of days go by without the Princess calling in on her mother.

Where the Princess Royal's grandmother, Queen Elizabeth the Queen Mother, is concerned the situation is different. They have never been particularly close, mainly because of the Queen Mother's widely known affection for Prince Charles, which seemed to exclude most of her other grandchildren. None the less, when the Princess Royal was asked to succeed her grandmother as Chancellor of London University, she readily agreed because, as she put it, 'You can't

141

really refuse her anything.' Anne is a dutiful granddaughter, and although one gets the impression that she knows she takes second place to her older brother, it doesn't particularly worry her.

The Royal Family are the most extraordinary self-protective group one could ever meet, and perhaps that is the source of their strength. They know that in the final analysis, they have each other. They appear to neither need, nor want, anyone else.

CHAPTER TEN

PETER AND ZARA—FAMILY LIFE

On her own admission the Princess Royal has never been a maternal woman. Even the birth of her first child, Peter, did little to change her views about motherhood.

Peter was born on 15 November 1977, a day after his parents' fourth wedding anniversary. He arrived on time, at 10.46 a.m. in the Lindo Wing of St Mary's Hospital, Paddington. He was the first Royal baby this century to have been born in hospital—all the others had first seen the light of day in a palace or castle—and he was the first grandchild of a British Sovereign to be born a commoner. Even so, he was fifth in the line of succession to the throne. Later, a number of Royal babies, including both the children of the Prince and Princess of Wales, would be born in St Mary's, but at that time it was a complete break with tradition—another first for Princess Anne.

The event which caused the Queen and the Duke of Edinburgh to become grandparents, and Queen Elizabeth the Queen Mother a great-grandmother, excited an enormous amount of interest at home and abroad. The Home Secretary, Mr Merlin Rees, was the first official to be informed of the birth, followed by the leaders of all the Commonwealth countries. The Prime Minister, James Callaghan, sent a telegram expressing the country's 'warmest congratulations'; Prince Charles, who was out hunting in Yorkshire, was told by short-wave radio, and at Gordonstoun two Royal pupils, Prince Andrew and Prince Edward, learned that they were uncles for the first time. Thousands of letters, telegrams and gifts poured into Buckingham Palace (the gifts later being given to local hospitals, as is the case with nearly everything that is sent unsolicited to the Royal Family). A predictably sour note was introduced by the well-known anti-Royalist MP Willie Hamilton, who said, 'How charming—another one on the payroll.'

Peter Phillips may have been an important addition to the Royal Family, but his parents were determined that he would be brought up in as ordinary a way as was possible for any child who has the Queen for grandmother. Apart from his christening, which took place in the Music Room at Buckingham Palace on 22 December 1977, and was conducted by the Archbishop of Canterbury, with the Prince of Wales standing as one of the godparents, Peter was not given any other special privileges because of his Royal connections. Princess Anne persuaded her mother not to give her grandson a title; his father didn't want one either, and even though the Queen and the Queen Mother were anxious to bestow one, they reluctantly agreed to Princess Anne's request. So he has remained plain Peter Phillips, without even an 'Hon' to add to his name. His mother believes that in this day and age a title would be more of a hindrance than an advantage as her children try to make their way in the world.

The birth made very little difference to the lifestyle of the Princess. As soon as she was fit again after the birth, she resumed her frantic workload and within weeks was back in the saddle training for events.

Peter was brought up by a nanny, a practical Yorkshire woman, Pat Moss, but unlike his future Royal cousins, Prince William and Prince Harry, he had no nursery footman, private maid or chauffeur. Peter also quickly got used to the idea of his parents being away for much of the time. Anne and Mark were not in any way neglectful parents, and when they were at home Mark in particular, an affectionate and doting father, spent a lot of time with their son. He used to be seen around the estate with the little boy in tow and often took him with him driving tractors and generally helping out on the farm. It was an ideal existence for any youngster and an excellent grounding for Peter's future character.

After attending the local village school at Minchinhampton and then Port Regis coeducational prep school, he went on to Gordonstoun, the public school hated by his godfather, Prince Charles. He was an instant success at the school and, following in the footsteps of his grandfather, Prince Philip, and his favourite uncle, Prince Edward (whom he calls 'Cled' from days when he found 'Uncle Edward' too much of a mouthful) he became Head Boy or Guardian as the position is called at Gordonstoun.

Like his father, Peter excelled at sports, playing in the school's first teams at rugby, hockey, cricket and football. These are the sports in which he describes himself as being 'really competitive'. To relax he plays squash and badminton, where he also admits he 'likes to win', while on the athletics field his speciality is the 110-metres hurdles. Physical education was one of his favourite subjects, in which he got an 'A' in his GCSE examinations, and he also took an A-level in PE in his final year.

Rugby is his number one sport, and to the delight of his mother, who is Patron of the Scottish Rugby Union, he gained his first Cap for Scotland playing in the Schools Rugby International against France in December 1995 at Murrayfield. His side lost but he played well enough to keep his place for the match against Wales and at both games his proud family were there to support him. One thing he could have done without though was the presence of nearly a hundred members of the media. It's hard enough to make your debut for your country under normal circumstances; the addition of so many cameras all focusing on you and you alone is something any eighteen-year-old would find a burden. He ended an outstanding season by being selected as part of the Scottish Schools Squad to tour South Africa in the summer of 1996.

Standing at 5 feet 11 inches and weighing 12

stone 3 pounds, Peter compares favourably in physical terms with some of the other male members of the Royal Family, but if he hopes to continue his rugby career at senior level, he needs a little more height and weight. It's a pity he's not as tall as his stepfather, who is 6 feet 3 inches.

Off the field, Peter is not averse to the usual antics of rugby players. On a tour of Australia with the Gordonstoun side he decided that it would be fun to get the team out of bed earlier than necessary when they were leaving to fly home. They were already scheduled to make a start at dawn, but he made an announcement that the team bus would leave thirty minutes early. After the celebrations of the night before, his team-mates were not amused.

On a personal level, Peter is a fairly down-to-earth young man who doesn't seem too concerned about his Royal relations or the fact that his grandmother is the most important woman in the land. At the same time, he is not above using his connections to enjoy some of the advantages his position allows. He occasionally takes a party of friends to Balmoral where they stay in Craigowan and sail or shoot. He also invites a friend or two to join him at Sandringham, with the Queen's approval. When he was younger his parents' old friend Jackie Stewart arranged for him to sample the delights of a Formula One racing car, and if he wanted to see or try anything unusual in the field of sports, there was often a world champion or equally qualified tutor on hand to introduce the youngster at the right level. And when he left Gordonstoun he joined Jackie Stewart's new Grand Prix motor racing team as a member of the

146

crew, to fill in the year before going to university.

So he's not exactly a run-of-the-mill commoner and even at school he was not considered to be the most outgoing or social of boys. As school Guardian he was popular, impartial and fair, but his immediate circle of friends was said to be fairly small and it was difficult to break in. Peter learned from his mother very early on not to make friends too easily and he was always wary of those he suspected might be seeking his companionship because of his position in the Royal Family.

Romantically his name has been linked with a couple of girls from Gordonstoun. One, Penny Taylor, who is two years older than him, taking up much of his spare time before she left. They once went on holiday together to Jamaica and Peter took the unusual step of talking to the Press about their relationship in an effort to protect her reputation. He said, 'We're good friends, that's all. I don't want anyone to get the wrong idea. And if anyone wants to know, we're not sleeping in the same room. We do know how to behave.'

The relationship with Penny did not survive once she had left Gordonstoun and in his final year his attention turned to a pretty blonde young lady. It was nothing serious and Peter, who has a normal young man's healthy interest in the opposite sex, is in no hurry to settle down.

His future career has yet to be decided. The Army is a possibility but in time he will almost certainly take up agriculture as he will eventually inherit the Gatcombe Park estate. Peter appears to have inherited most of his characteristics from his father. He is nowhere as forceful or outspoken as his mother, but, just as with his father, it is impossible to force him to do something he does not want to do, and he has Mark's quiet determination and steely ambition.

The Princess Royal's daughter, Zara, four years younger than her brother, was born on 15 May 1981. Her mother had wanted the birth to take place at home, or at least in Windsor Castle which was not too far from London if an emergency arose, but the Royal gynaecologist, George Pinker, persuaded her to return to St Mary's Hospital where she occupied the same suite as she had when Peter was born. It was just as well, as Zara chose to arrive a week late. She weighed in at 8 pounds 1 ounce and the birth was witnessed by a reluctant Mark Phillips, who later said, 'Yes, I was present at the birth, but I wouldn't recommend it to other fathers.'

The choice of name was unusual for a member of the Royal Family, but was suggested by Prince Charles. Princess Anne told me, 'The baby made a rather sudden and positive arrival and my brother thought that Zara [a Greek biblical name meaning "bright as the dawn"] was appropriate.' She said that neither she nor Mark had heard of it before, but one of her most senior Ladies-in-Waiting, the Hon. Shân Legge-Bourke (mother of the now famous Tiggy) also had a daughter named Zara, so in fact it is highly unlikely that the Princess had not heard the name mentioned.

If Peter's birth had not altered the Princess's attitude towards motherhood, Zara's arrival on the domestic scene at Gatcombe certainly seems to have done the trick, even though Anne's attempts to play down the joys of having a baby included her remarks about pregnancy being an occupational hazard of being married, and something of a bore. Shortly after Zara was born I was at Gatcombe discussing with the Princess a television film I was making about her life and work. She asked me if I would like to see the baby, and when we walked into the conservatory where Zara was sleeping in her pram, there was no doubting the maternal pride and love that shone from her face. One could even go so far as to say that she was besotted with her new baby and any maternal feelings that may have been lying dormant—or at least, kept deliberately hidden—suddenly leaped into life. It was a moving moment to see the enormous amount of pleasure the so-called hard-bitten Princess got from seeing one very small child.

Zara—her full names are Zara Anne Elizabeth—was christened in the Private Chapel at Windsor Castle on 27 July 1981 by the Dean, the Rt Rev'd Michael Mann, a former fellow officer of Mark Phillips in 1st The Queen's Dragoon Guards. Among the godparents were Prince Andrew, Helen, the wife of former racing driver Jackie Stewart, and Andrew Parker Bowles (this was long before his ex-wife brought the family name such notoriety).

As Zara grew up she quickly became her mother's daughter. Physically there is a strong resemblance and mentally they appear to be completely in tune. And whereas, in the early days, Mark was rarely seen around Gatcombe without Peter in tow, Zara was similarly never very far from Anne's side. Both children were introduced to riding at an early age and by the time they were four years old, were as comfortable in the saddle as they were on foot. Zara is also said to have inherited many of the characteristics of her paternal grandmother, the late Mrs Anne Phillips, one of which is her dislike of the limelight.

As Peter Phillips matured, his sporting interests took off on the rugby field, but Zara followed in her mother's footsteps. She showed early promise as a rider and won a number of competitions in Pony Club events, much to her mother's delight. So far there is no sign of her early passion for the sport cooling.

Both Anne and Mark have said that while they would be pleased if either of their children wanted to take up Three-Day Eventing seriously, they would not push them and want them to be allowed to develop at their own pace. They realize how difficult it is for a son or daughter to succeed in a field where their parents have already reached the highest level. With both Anne and Mark achieving Olympic standard and representing their country, it is never going to be easy for Zara to follow them. Inevitably, she is going to be compared with her mother, who won the European Three-Day Championship (which made her virtually World Champion) at twenty-one, and whenever she competes, even at local shows, the spotlight is always on her. But Zara doesn't appear to worry too much about the attention she receives and, unlike her brother, she has inherited her mother's outspokenness and forthright attitudes. If she has something to say, she says it, regardless of who is around and irrespective of their rank.

Her fellow pupils at school say Zara mixes well and doesn't throw her weight around, but she's no shrinking violet either. Her education has mirrored that of her brother: village school followed by Port

Regis prep school and then Gordonstoun, where she is in her third year. Zara likes school and joins in most of the activities. She's good at swimming and sailing, but says she doesn't mind a bit the fact that the spartan regime involving cold baths, summer and winter, has been relaxed. When Anne and Mark were deciding how their children were to be educated, they knew that whatever they chose, someone would criticize them: it was a 'no-win' situation. If they sent Peter and Zara to expensive private schools they would be accused of being 'elitist', and if they decided on the state system, others would claim they were merely trying to curry favour.

In talking about the situation that faced them more than ten years ago, the Princess unconsciously anticipated the problems that have confronted several senior political figures much more recently, when she said, 'You must do what you think is best for your child . . . I read about the controversy Labour politicians get involved in when they send their children to private schools . . . That's part of what freedom of choice in this country is about. When a Labour politician is known to be sending one of his children to private school, one half of the country says, "Fair enough" and the other half says "You shouldn't." Some people might say about us, "Why don't they send them to State schools?" . . . others might say, "Why are they in the State system when they can afford to have their children educated privately?" . . . I think the child must come first . . . you have to work out what's best for him or her.'

When she has finished at Gordonstoun, Zara will probably go on to university and then find a job. There is no question of her or Peter taking a public role within the Royal Family. Her mother believes that the fact that their grandmother happens to be Queen does not make them Royal, and they will be required to find suitable careers away from the limelight. The problem is that while the Princess Royal likes to consider her children to be non-Royal, no one else is ever going to allow them to forget that their grandmother is Queen and they are in direct line of descent from Queen Victoria. It's a millstone that they will have to carry for the rest of their lives. They are still numbers nine and ten respectively in the line of succession to the throne, ahead of Princess Margaret and the Dukes of Gloucester and Kent, even if neither is known as a Royal Highness. When they marry, the guest list will include the Queen (or King if it's many years hence), and Royalty will inevitably feature largely in all family functions. Doors will open because of who their mother and grandparents are, and people will try to cultivate them in the hope of currying favour with the Royal Family.

The 'no-nonsense' attitude of the Princess Royal which has been so influential so far in their upbringing, will stand them in good stead in their future lives, however. She knows they are going to have to stand on their own in the twenty-first century and she welcomes the fact that they will never have the disadvantage of being called Prince or Princess.

Peter and Zara are seemingly unaffected by their parents' divorce and their mother's remarriage and they enjoy a mature relationship with their mother, father and stepfather. Whatever else Anne and

Mark may have got wrong in their personal lives, they certainly appear to have made a pretty good job of raising their children.

CHAPTER ELEVEN

WORLD TRAVELLER

In the twenty-eight years that the Princess Royal has been carrying out public duties, she has crisscrossed the world several times and visited little-known countries previously unthought of in the Royal schedule: Upper Volta, Siberia, Burma, war-torn Beirut, wherever she has felt there was a need, or she might do some good, she has gone unhesitatingly, if at times a little apprehensively.

In December 1991, she became the first member of the Royal Family to visit Kuwait since the Gulf War, cramming eight engagements into each twenty-four hours. This was straight after returning from an exhausting trip to Mauritius where she examined cyclone damage on an offshore island.

The previous year she had achieved another first when she became the first Royal to make an official visit to the Soviet Union since the Revolution and the assassination of the Tsar and his family in 1918. The Princess had earlier travelled to Kiev as part of the British Equestrian Team for the European Championships, but this was the first official visit, with all the pomp and ceremony that implied. She met the man who had defeated her for the Nobel Peace Prize, President Mikhail Gorbachev, and travelled 7,000 miles within the Soviet Union in two weeks, flying between Moscow, Siberia, Turkmenistan and back to Kiev.

In 1993 Tim Laurence found out what it was like to be welcomed as a member of the Royal Family, when he accompanied his wife to Mongolia and Uzbekistan on their first official trip abroad together. Instead of having to help with the arrangements for other people, he found that the Household were taking care of everything for him. It must have been a strange, initially slightly off-putting experience.

In the early years of her foreign trips Princess Anne was often the focus of attention and her every word and action was scrutinized by the media. In 1963, during a visit to Australia with her mother, she shouted out, 'I can't see in this bloody wind.' The reporters loved it. And on her first overseas trip alone, in 1969, when she went to Germany to visit her regiment 14/20th King's Hussars, she gave the media plenty to photograph and write about when she drove a fifty-two-ton Chieftain tank—appropriately named Princess Anne—over three miles of rough ground. On that same trip she also scored eleven bull's-eyes when she tried her hand at firing a sub-machine-gun from the hip. Her later journeys to foreign parts were deliberately more low-key as she worked on behalf of the Save the Children Fund, of which she has been President for more than twenty-five years.

These days the Princess Royal's schedule reads like a workaholic's diary. Rarely is there a day—or even an hour—when she is not doing something. An excellent example of the way in which she manages to fill every waking moment is encapsulated in the list of her engagements between 30 January and 3 February 1996. On those dates the Princess Royal paid her first visit to the Falkland Islands (the first by a member of the Royal Family for five years) during which she met 912 people (the entire population is only 2,000, with 1,700 living in the capital, Stanley), attended receptions, lunches and dinners—and two functions described as 'Smokos'—toured the battlefields of the 1982 campaign, paid a private tribute to the men who died there, went to a race meeting, presented prizes, laid a foundation stone, talked with servicemen and their families, watched how some of the islanders earn a living by knitting, sat in while children had lessons at school, and saw sheltered housing accommodation in one of the island's hospitals. The days began before eight and most nights she did not get to bed before midnight.

A look at the official programme for the visit reveals the extent of the detail that is involved in a typical Royal tour, or at least where the Princess Royal is involved.

MONDAY, 29 JANUARY 1996
22.45 hrs   The Princess Royal and her party, private secretary, Lt Col Peter Gibbs, personal bodyguard, Inspector Tomlinson, and dresser, Mrs Rosie Farnworth, leave RAF Brize Norton in Oxfordshire, in an RAF Tristar for the overnight flight to the Falklands via Ascension Island. Air Commodore the Hon. Timothy Elworthy, Captain of The Royal Flight, also accompanied the Princess.

155

07.30 hrs   Arrive at Ascension Island for one-and-a-half-hour stop, departing at 09.00 hrs.

12.30 hrs   The Governor and official 'Greeters' leave for Mount Pleasant airfield to meet the Princess.

14.05 hrs   Tristar arrives (on time) at Falkland Islands. The official party waiting to greet her is: The Governor and his wife (Mr and Mrs Richard Ralph), CBFFI and Mrs Backus, Councillor William (known as Bill) Luxton, Councillor Norma Edwards, Clerk of Councils Claudette Anderson. This meeting takes exactly 12 minutes and then the greeting party returns to Stanley and the Princess's dresser (Mrs Farnworth) with all the luggage is driven by Land-Rover to Government House where HRH is staying. Meanwhile the official programme gets underway immediately. The Princess does not want a rest period to get over the long flight.

14.17 hrs   Leave apron for Headquarters, British Forces Falkland Islands (HQBFFI) in two vehicles.

14.25 hrs   Arrive Theatre Operation Centre (HQBFFI). Meet Deputy Commander British Forces Falkland Island Group, Group Captain Philip Owen, RAF, Chief Staff Officer (Operations), Commander Clive Murgatroyd, MBE, RN, and duty personnel.

14.45 hrs   Visit Joint Communications Unit Falkland Islands (within Theatre

Operations Centre) and meet Royal Signals (of which she is Colonel-in-Chief), Royal Navy and Royal Air Force personnel. The Princess always insists that on these visits she does not want to meet only the senior officers and civic dignitaries.

15.00 hrs Leave HQBFFI.

15.05 hrs Arrive Falkland Islands Logistics Unit (FILU) to meet Royal Logistic Corps personnel.

15.30 hrs Leave FILU.

15.45 hrs Arrive Resident Rapier Squadron (RRS) at Poon Hill. Meet RRS personnel.

16.05 hrs Leave RRS.

16.15 hrs Arrive 1312 Flight (Hercules) to meet RAF Lyneham personnel. (RAF Lyneham is the nearest RAF station to the Princess's home at Gatcombe and she is their Honorary Air Commodore.)

16.35 hrs Leave 1312 Flight.

16.40 hrs Arrive Bristows Helicopters to meet Bristows personnel.

16.45 hrs HRH and Royal party leave by helicopter for Government House.

17.00 hrs Arrive football field, Stanley (West End) and walk to Government House to be met by Governor and his wife.

19.30 hrs Quiet supper at Government House.

This was after a 7,000-mile, twenty-two-hour flight in an RAF Tristar with virtually no sleep apart from a few snatched hours and no opportunity to rest before starting out on the day's programme.

The following day was just as crowded.

WEDNESDAY, 31 JANUARY—EAST FALKLANDS DAY
The Princess was woken at 7 a.m. with just an hour to bathe, breakfast and get ready for the first engagement.

08.05 hrs   Leave Government House on foot for Liberation Monument.

08.15 hrs   Walk to Secretariat for Falkland Islands Government briefing in Liberation Room. (The Governor, Chief Executive and Financial Secretary, to give the briefing.) Princess to sign visitors' book.

08.45 hrs   Walk from Secretariat to King Edward Memorial Hospital to visit chalet in Sheltered Housing complex. (The Princess to be met by Dr Roger Diggle, Chief Medical Officer, Mrs Candy Blakely, Hospital Administrator and Mrs Connie May-Warden.)

08.50 hrs   Walk from Sheltered Housing complex to Day Care Centre at King Edward Memorial Hospital to meet residents.

09.15 hrs   Visit the wards and meet patients in the hospital. (Sign visitors' book.)

09.25 hrs   Walk from King Edward Memorial Hospital to Falklander Workshop (knitting).

09.30 hrs   Arrive Falklander Workshop. (Met by Mr Ian Dempster, Assistant General Manager, Falkland Islands Development Corporation.) Presentation of Falklander sweater to the Princess

158

Royal, HRH to sign visitors' book.

09.50 hrs Walk to cathedral.

09.55 hrs Arrive at cathedral to be met by Canon Stephen Palmer and Church Wardens—Mrs Marj McPhee, Mr Les Halliday, and Mr Desmond King—Archbishop of Canterbury's representative.

10.00 hrs Short service (which includes recorded greeting from Archbishop of Canterbury).

10.15 hrs Sign visitors' book in Vestry.

10.20 hrs Proceed to Paris Hall and unveil plaque. Meet the donors and contractor.

10.40 hrs Leave Paris Hall—see Whale Bone Arch and return to Government House.

11.20 hrs Leave for Stanley Airport.

11.30 hrs Arrive Stanley Airport. (Met by Mr Gerald Cheek—Director of Civil Aviation, Mr Vernon Steen—General Manager, Falkland Islands Government Air Service.)

11.40 hrs Fly to San Carlos. (2 Islander aircraft designated A & B. Aircraft B to arrive at destinations before aircraft A.) Her Royal Highness the Princess Royal (A), Governor (A) and Mrs Ralph (B), Lt Col Gibbs—Private Secretary (B), Air Commodore Elworthy (A), Inspector Tomlinson—[Bodyguard] (A), Claudette Anderson (B), Mr N. Clark (B).

12.00 hrs Arrive San Carlos. Meet Mr Pat Short and Mr Adrian Minnell who look after the Cemetery. Walk to the British Military Cemetery and lay wreath. Sign

159

visitors' book. Drive to Blue Beach Lodge. Met by William and Linda Anderson, Owners of the Lodge (presented with bouquet). Meet and have Smoko with residents from San Carlos and surrounding farms (sign visitors' book at Lodge).

12.45 hrs Leave San Carlos Airfield in 2 Islander aircraft.

13.00 hrs Arrive Goose Green to be met by Tony and June McMullen (Farm Manager) and Brook and Eileen Hardcastle (HRH to shearing shed in McMullens' vehicle).

13.15 hrs Visit shearing shed and observe shearing in process (meet Mr Neil McKay, shearing contractor).

13.30 hrs Visit Battlefield and Memorial to Lt Col H. Jones VC (Guide: Mr Brook Hardcastle), HRH in Hardcastles' vehicle.

14.00 hrs Opportunity for Royal Party to freshen up at the home of Tony and June McMullen.

14.10 hrs Walk from McMullens' home to Community Centre.

14.15 hrs Drinks and buffet lunch at Goose Green Community Centre to meet East Falkland Residents (Tony and June McMullen to make introductions).

15.15 hrs Leave Goose Green green by helicopter (Bristows). Mr Clark to return to Stanley.

15.45 hrs Arrive Sea Lion Lodge—Sea Lion Island. (Met by David and Pat Gray—Owners of the Lodge.)

16.00 hrs Tour of beaches and penguin rookeries with Mr Gray.

20.00 hrs Dinner (no other guests).

THURSDAY, 1 FEBRUARY—WEST FALKLANDS DAY

09.30 hrs Leave Sea Lion Lodge with baggage by helicopter for Fox Bay East.

09.45 hrs (FIGAS [Falkland Island General Aviation Service] Islanders arrive Fox Bay Airstrip with Mr Clark.)

10.00 hrs Arrive Fox Bay East to be met by Councillor Norma Edwards and Mr Ken Halliday (Village Agent). (Mrs Farnworth to return MPA on Bristows Helicopter with baggage.)

10.05 hrs Visit Fox Bay Mill (Guides: Richard and Grizelda Cockwell—Directors and Shareholders).

10.45 hrs Smoko in Community Centre with West Falkland residents.

11.30 hrs Leave for Fox Bay Airstrip in 2 Land-Rovers.

11.45 hrs Take off for Hill Cove in 2 Islander aircraft with same seating as previous day.

12.15 hrs Land Hill Cove. Met by Tim and Sally Blake.

12.20 hrs Walk to stable and see working horses.

12.30 hrs Lunch with Tim and Sally Blake and other West Falkland residents. Sign visitors' book.

14.00 hrs Take off for Port Howard.

14.20 hrs Land Port Howard to be met by Rodney and Carol Lee and Robin Lee (farm owners). Dog-handling display by Mr Les Morrison. Smoko at Port Howard Social Club with Community Presentation of sweater to HRH by Eddie and Ann Chandler of A & E Knitwear, Port Howard.

16.00 hrs Take off for Stanley.

16.40 hrs Land Stanley Airport.

17.00 hrs Back in Government House.

19.00 hrs FIG reception in Town Hall for Islanders.

19.10 hrs Leave Government House for FIG reception in Town Hall.

19.15 hrs Arrival of HRH at Town Hall.
Legislature Dinner at Malvina House Hotel.
(Presentation of gift to HRH and a few words before dinner in Beagle Bar.)

FRIDAY, 2 FEBRUARY

09.00 hrs Leave football field by helicopter to west of Tumbledown Mountain for Battlefield tour. (HRH and party to walk the route of the Battle.)

12.00 hrs Pick-up from Moody Brook to return Government House.

12.20 hrs Lunch at Government House.

15.15 hrs Leave Government House for junior school (Governor and Mrs Ralph and Clerk of Councils to accompany).

15.20 hrs Arrive junior school to be met by Mrs Phyllis Rendell, Director of Education, Mrs Jean Smith, Head Teacher. Her Royal Highness to lay foundation stone. (Schoolchildren will be present in

162

playground.)

15.45 hrs	Leave junior school.
15.50 hrs	Arrive at Tim Blake's paddock. (Meet Mr Owen Summers and see Thyer, the Stanley Sports Association stallion given by Sheikh Maktoum Al Maktoum.)
15.55 hrs	Leave Tim Blake's paddock for museum.
16.00 hrs	Arrive museum to be met by Mr John Smith (Curator). Sign visitors' book. (Meet Mike [artist] and Claire Peake.)
16.55 hrs	Leave museum.
17.00 hrs	Arrive Stanley Racecourse. Met by Chairman of Stanley Sports Association Mr Mike Summers and members of Committee. 3 races—17.05, 17.35 ending with Princess Royal's Plate at 18.00 hrs. (HRH to observe races and present 1st prizes.)
18.20 hrs	Return to Government House.
20.00 hrs	Governor's Farewell Dinner at Government House.

SATURDAY, 3 FEBRUARY

09.00 hrs	Baggage and Mrs Farnworth leave Government House.
10.30 hrs	Royal Party leaves football field (west end by Government House) by helicopter. (Councillor Richard Stevens and Councillor Sharon Halford farewell from Government House.) Governor and Mrs Ralph, Clerk of Councils on helicopter with Royal Party.
11.00 hrs	Depart Falkland Islands by Royal Air Force Tristar. Farewell party: Governor

and Mrs Ralph, Commodore and Mrs Backus, Clerk of Councils. (Governor and Mrs Ralph and Clerk of Councils return to Stanley.)

21.00 hrs Arrive Ascension Island.

22.40 hrs Depart Ascension Island.

This is just the bare outline of the five-day programme, which, of course, gives no indication of the amount of work that had gone into preparing it. Lieutenant Colonel Gibbs had flown to the Falklands several weeks before the visit and walked every step of the proposed routes. People who were to be presented to HRH were seen and biographical notes taken so that she would know not only who she was meeting, but also something of their background and what part they played in the life of the islands. On his return to Buckingham Palace he prepared a draft programme. Once the programme had been agreed—and approved by the Princess—it was circulated to all those who needed to know its contents, with a photographically reduced copy which she could slip into a handbag or pocket.

The Princess had given her usual instructions that her visit was to be low-key, and this applied to her travel arrangements as well as accommodation and hospitality in the Falklands. Peter Gibbs did not have to decide whether the party would fly Concorde or merely first-class, as the flight was on an ordinary RAF troop-carrying aircraft, which also carried vital supplies for the islands' garrison.

Her Royal Highness's accommodation was not a specially prepared luxurious suite in a five-star

164

hotel, but a basic though comfortable room in Government House. When she went to pay tribute to the 255 British servicemen who lost their lives during the Falklands Campaign, there were no bands playing or large crowds watching. Instead she went alone, dressed simply and practically for the weather in cap, short jacket and trousers, and stood in silent respect to the war heroes, including Lieutenant Colonel H. Jones, who was killed in the action which won him the posthumous Victoria Cross. The occasion lacked nothing in dignity through the absence of ceremony. Face to face with one of the saddest memorials in recent military history, the Princess behaved with impeccable dignity and discipline. Her control was absolute, instilled through years of training which few can match. Her composure did not slip for a moment as her thoughts went back fourteen years to those days when so many young men lost their lives on that bleak battlefield. If there were any tears, they were shed in private.

When the Princess Royal visited the tiny hospital and junior school, there were no photo-opportunities to be exploited. She did not pick up and cuddle any of the children she met, still sticking to her old principle of 'not doing stunts'. And although chauffeur-driven cars were available, she preferred walking where it was practicable, and Land-Rovers where it wasn't.

Claudette Anderson, the islands' Clerk of the Councils, was one of those in the official party to welcome the Princess and to accompany her on a number of visits around the islands. She remembers her first impression: 'We were all a little apprehensive at first about meeting a member of the Royal Family, but from the moment she stepped off the aircraft she was relaxed and friendly. Throughout the four days she was here she could not have been more approachable and down-to-earth. And one of the things I remember her saying was how "British" the Falklands are and how friendly all the people seemed to be.'

There is a tradition in the Falklands that everything stops at 10.30 in the morning for what they call a 'Smoko'. Claudette Anderson described it as a 'cuppa and a fag'. On the farms all work stops and the men and women go home or to one of the barns for a twenty-minute break. The Princess attended a couple of these 'Smokos' and thoroughly enjoyed herself, although, unlike the others, she did not have to provide her own tea and sandwiches—in honour of her visit, the women of the farms laid on something a bit special. But it was the complete lack of formality that appealed to Her Royal Highness, and the way she joined in made for a very relaxed gathering.

Norma Edwards is a Falkland Islands councillor who as a member of the Government was involved in the official reception party for the Princess and several other less formal functions as well. Her impression of the Princess was typical of that of many of the islanders: 'I couldn't believe that when she walked off the aircraft she didn't want to go and lie down for a couple of hours. She looked as fresh as if she had just stepped out of a shower and she was anxious to start the programme immediately. She was utterly charming and the easiest of any VIPs that we have had to entertain.'

When the Princess visited a knitwear workshop it was obvious to Mrs Edwards that this was not merely a courtesy call, 'She had done her homework and her penetrating and intelligent questions showed how much she knew of the industry.' Another aspect of the Princess's character showed when she attended a reception at the social club. A private yacht had anchored the previous evening, and three of its crew, two Americans and a Canadian, dropped in to the affair. They were warmly welcomed and joined in the festivities, being delighted and surprised at finding themselves in the company of Royalty. The Princess did not object, even though the party was meant for the local residents.

Mrs Edwards added that everyone was astounded by the Princess's stamina. 'She went for a walk every morning before breakfast and throughout the day she showed no sign of tiredness, even when the rest of us were weakening a bit.'

Richard Ralph had been Governor of the Falkland Islands for only three weeks when his Royal guest descended on him. It could have been daunting, particularly as he remembered a previous encounter with the Princess, in Harare, Zimbabwe, in the early eighties. At that time she was going through one of her periodic battles with the Press, and the Governor recalled a 'certain snappishness' with one or two members of the press corps. So it came as a delightful surprise and relief to find that in 1996 the Princess Royal could not have been a more agreeable guest. 'The idea of having a senior member of the Royal Family staying with you in your house can be a bit unnerving, but she could not have been easier. From the moment we first met, she put my wife and me at ease, and as soon as the official part of the day's events were over, she relaxed totally and displayed a marvellous sense of humour. What could have been a very formal and stuffy affair turned into a damn good party.'

The Governor and his wife, Margaret, gave up their bedroom for the Princess. 'It's the only one in the house with its own bathroom. She didn't ask for it and I'm sure she would have been happy with whatever arrangements we'd made but we wanted to make her comfortable and I think we managed it. There were no special demands for food. She enjoyed simple meals and even on the last night when we gave an official farewell dinner in her honour, it was not the sort of grand formal banquet she might be used to. There were no speeches, evening dress was not worn—the men came in ordinary suits—and even though we had the best silver out, everything was relaxed and informal, just sixteen guests, so she could meet them all. It was a lovely atmosphere.'

Just before the Princess arrived a television team from Argentina had applied for permission to cover the visit. All such applications are considered by the islands' Executive Council, which is chaired by the Governor. It was decided to refuse permission on the grounds that the islanders, being somewhat undemonstrative, might have turned out in embarrassingly small numbers, or been rather silent, and the fear was that this might have been twisted to suggest the islanders were anti-British monarchy, or just plain apathetic about the United Kingdom connection. As it happened, there was a very large crowd at the airport when the Princess

168

Royal arrived. They were all keen to see her, but such is the character of the islanders that there was no shouting or screaming—just the warmest and most courteous of welcomes.

Richard Ralph also said it was obvious that the Princess had done her homework thoroughly. 'What impressed the farmers was her knowledge of horses and sheep and also of many of the problems they faced. It wasn't simply a question of her merely being polite; she really wanted to know, and her comments made them realize that she knew what she was talking about. People here are not flash or demonstrative, and they don't always take to strangers easily. But the Princess clicked immediately. I think they saw in her what people used to expect of a member of the Royal Family before all the unpleasantness occurred involving certain junior members in recent times.' When she met members of the British garrison stationed in the Falklands, she displayed a remarkable knowledge of military affairs and terminology, which put her in their good books straight away. Of course, she has been associated with all three Services for many years, and one of her regiments, the Royal Signals, were among the first to land in the Falkland Islands after the Argentine invasion.

Richard Ralph says that although Her Royal Highness 'does the "tiara stuff" beautifully when required', the main impression he, and his fellow Falklanders, had was of an 'unfussy' woman who demanded the minimum of protocol and was at her happiest and most successful in 'jeans and a Barbour'. 'But', he added, 'one was always aware of who she is. It's not anything she does in particular, it's just an aura she has that makes her stand out

169

from everyone else.' He was also impressed by how fit she is. 'When she went up Mount Tumbledown, the scene of some of the most bitter fighting in 1982, she scrambled up rockfaces like a mountain goat, setting a cracking pace that left some of us in the party gasping to keep up.' The Governor said he believed she had a good time in the Falkland Islands and in turn 'She was great value.'

Patrick Watts is something of an institution in the Falklands. He is the leading radio personality for the Falkland Islands Broadcasting Service and he had interviewed all the prominent people who had visited the islands before the Princess Royal came. 'I had spoken to Prince Philip, who was not the easiest man I have ever met, Prince Edward and Margaret Thatcher, so I was more than slightly surprised and disappointed when I was told that the Princess Royal did not give interviews. I didn't give up but kept on and on and eventually I was told to report to Government House with a list of questions. This is obviously not the ideal way to conduct an interview but beggars can't be choosers, so off I went with my tape-recorder. I had previously met the Princess briefly on the Isle of Wight in 1993 and when I was presented to her I mentioned this. She was kind enough to say she remembered it—even if she didn't. We started on the interview and straight away she made life very easy for me. She didn't stick to the prepared questions at all; she volunteered comments and opinions of her own and she was one of the easiest people to speak to I've ever met. There was a tremendous warmth about her. It was towards the end of her visit and she was relaxed and obviously pleased with her reception.' Watts asked her why she had not accepted the offer to ride a horse named after her in the Princess Royal Stakes at the Island's racecourse. Her reply was succinct and to the point, 'Because no one told me about the offer.' Still, she had stayed to present all the prizes at the event when the programme said she would be there only for the big race itself.

Patrick Watts said that one of the moments he will most cherish about her visit—apart from his scoop interview—was at the race meeting, when Her Royal Highness's host suggested they should leave the VIP enclosure and go to meet some more of the people. The Princess Royal turned to him and said, 'I've got a better idea, let's go the other way and meet the horses instead.'

Norma Edwards summed up the feelings of all the Falkland Islanders when she said, 'There's no doubt that in Royal terms, we got the best of the bargain. Argentina got Diana—we got Anne. And somehow we know this was not just another Royal "one-off" visit. She'll be back and we'll be waiting for her.'

CHAPTER TWELVE

THE OFFICE

If either the *Daily Telegraph* or the *Daily Express*, the two newspapers which are delivered daily to Gatcombe Park, does not arrive promptly on the doorstep, the person who chases up the newsagent is Mrs Margaret Hammond, the Princess Royal's secretary based at Gatcombe. She was for many years Mark's assistant but when he left she stayed on to work for the Princess and is now responsible for much of the day-to-day running of the house.

The Hon. Mrs Louloudis, the former Maddy Dillon, daughter of the Irish peer, the late Viscount Dillon, is another member of the compact support team that handles the busy programme of the busiest member of the Royal Family. She had been working as social secretary to the late Jack Heinz, of the famous beans family, when a mutual friend she shared with Victoria Legge-Bourke told her of a vacancy in the Royal Household, though not whom she might be working for at that time. After an interview with the Princess Royal, 'at which we discussed just about everything but the job itself', she found herself installed as Assistant Private Secretary and one of the few female 'Members' of the Royal Household. One of her prime responsibilities is looking after the household accounts. This is only one of her many duties but occupies a considerable amount of her time. Her work is conducted mainly from her office in Buckingham Palace, though she does visit Gatcombe about once every three weeks. If repairs or decoration are required at the house, she will contact the contractors and agree with them the amount of work to be done.

Looking at the number of engagements that the Princess undertakes throughout the year, and the 300-plus organizations with which she is associated, it would be easy to imagine that there is a vast machinery behind her, with banks of clerical staff, administrators and other officials, all geared up to smooth her way. So it comes as something of a surprise to the first-time visitor to her Buckingham

Palace office, in what used to be the Palace schoolroom, to find just five full-time staff.

The man with overall charge of the Princess Royal's public life is her Private Secretary, Lieutenant Colonel Peter Gibbs, a sixty-three-year-old former Coldstream Guards officer who has been her senior Aide since 1982. Peter Gibbs is large, friendly and highly efficient, and was secretly amused to see himself described by a lady journalist as 'a huge bear of a man'. The only male in the office, he has a reputation for being easy-going but with a fearsome bark when things go wrong. The ladies regard him with affection, but only his chief assistant, Maddy Louloudis, calls him by his Christian name. To the others he is 'The Colonel'. This is because he and Mrs Louloudis are both Members of the Royal Household, while the three secretaries in the outer office are Officials. They eat in different dining-rooms, do not act as Ladies-in-Waiting (as Maddy does occasionally), and a definite line divides the two categories, outside the office at least; inside there is an easy informality between all the players in the Princess Royal's team.

One of the Princess Royal's secretaries is a Royal Navy non-commissioned officer on secondment, and another, Jane Hambling, originally came to the Princess Royal as a temporary worker under the Youth Training Scheme and proved such a success that she was asked to return as a permanent member of the private staff. Between them the five organize the public life of the Princess Royal, handling up to 25,000 items of mail every year, every one of which receives an answer by return. Lieutenant Colonel

173

Gibbs has one inflexible rule and that is that all the 'in-trays' must be cleared every night before anyone leaves the office.

They make plentiful use of the telephone and facsimile machines, often having to explain as tactfully as possible why the Princess cannot attend a dinner for a group of old age pensioners who 'would simply love to meet her' or speak at a charity function because 'The Princess of Wales has turned us down'. Buckingham Palace does not have a cross-reference system when it comes to Royal engagements. So unless it is known that perhaps two of them are travelling in the same direction on the same day and it might be convenient to share a helicopter, individuals rarely know what the rest of the family is doing. And if a request is received for one member of the Royal Family to attend a function which they are unable to accept, the invitation is never passed on to someone else. As one of the Queen's Private Secretaries dryly remarked, 'We are not in the business of "Rent-a-Royal".' It might seem a haphazard way of working when you have half a dozen Royals all carrying out public duties in various parts of the world, but it does seem to work, and there have rarely been occasions when two of them have appeared in the same town or city on the same day.

The Private Secretary is the chief executive of the office. He sees every piece of correspondence that goes in or out and he is responsible for ensuring that the Princess Royal's programme runs smoothly and efficiently. He does not have anything to do with her private life. He does not socialize with her and they do not talk about private matters except where they might affect her public role. For example, Peter Gibbs was not the first person to learn that his boss was getting married to Tim Laurence, in his opinion quite rightly so. It was none of his business. The Princess deliberately kept him in the dark so that he would not be put in the position of having to deny anything, and that suits both of them very well. As he says, 'Our relationship is purely professional. I am her Private Secretary and when we speak, either in person or on the telephone, there is never any frivolous small-talk. I wouldn't dream of ringing her up just for a chat. She would think I had gone off my head—and she'd be quite right.'

Conversely, the Princess would never agree to an engagement without informing Lieutenant Colonel Gibbs. She knows the rules as well as he and sticks to them rigidly. You would never have the kind of situation that arose in the household of Diana, Princess of Wales, where she did television interviews and accepted engagements without the knowledge of her private office. That would be unthinkable in the Princess Royal's eyes and an unforgivable lapse of the good manners she shows towards her Private Secretary.

Peter Gibbs lives in a remote area of Devon, from where he commutes weekly to his office on the second-floor front of Buckingham Palace, overlooking the forecourt with a magnificent view of the Changing of the Guard. He also has the use of a Grace and Favour apartment in St James's Palace where his immediate neighbours are Princess Alexandra and her husband, Sir Angus Ogilvy.

The Colonel's office is next door to the Princess's sitting-room and it can be quite disconcerting to a first-time visitor sitting in his room when she pops her head around the door to ask him something. There is no great formality and she will usually acknowledge the visitor without waiting to be introduced.

The Colonel shares his office with whichever of the Ladies-in-Waiting happens to be on duty. But they only use their desk to write their 'bread-and-butter' thank-you letters on behalf of the Princess following an engagement so are rarely in the office for any length of time.

Between this office and Maddy Louloudis's next door is a small hatch through which the Personal Secretary and his Assistant talk to each other, while the general office is on Mrs Louloudis's other side. This is the 'boiler-room' where all the correspondence and files are kept and where the most important piece of equipment is said to be the kettle. Visitors to the Princess Royal's office are never offered a whisky or gin, but coffee or tea is always available.

The office is practically self-contained, with its own bathroom and lavatory just along the corridor, and outside in the hallway you will often see piles of suitcases, boxes and hanging wardrobes, particularly if the Princess is about to set off on one of her overseas trips, or has just returned from one. She is often given presents by her hosts abroad and each one is listed and catalogued. This is the system that applies with every member of the Royal Family and occasionally the ingenuity of the household is tasked to the limit trying to find suitable resting homes for some of the presents. The Queen has been given live baby crocodiles, the Duke of Edinburgh necklaces made of whale's teeth, and the Princess Royal a variety of large stuffed animals.

Because of the way in which the Princess's office is organized, and its location in relation to the other Household offices in the Palace, there is very little communication with the rest of the Household. Peter Gibbs might slip along to have a chat with Captain Neil Blair, his opposite number in the Duke of York's office on the same floor, but unless he is having lunch in the Household dining-room, he rarely has occasion to speak to his other colleagues. Similarly, the girls in the office tend to keep to themselves and do not mix with the others in the Duke of Edinburgh's office nearby or in Prince Edward's, unless there is a special reason.

The Princess Royal works out her programme for the year at least six months in advance, with some engagements—those involving travel to distant countries in difficult conditions where the Foreign Office and several overseas official departments may be involved—sometimes taking over a year to arrange. She and Peter Gibbs will sit down twice a year, in June and December, and plan the next six months from the letters that have arrived. He will already have sorted them into different categories showing the various priorities.

The Princess Royal has her own set of questions which she applies to every request for her presence. She wants to know, 'Why do they want me? What good will it do if I accept? Have I been there before, if so, when, and was it a success?' The Princess has a practical mind and a phenomenal memory, so she will often decline an invitation because she remembers going somewhere, or close by, fairly recently—too recently, in her view, to warrant a second visit. She knows that familiarity has a tendency to devalue the currency. She also tries to combine a number of engagements if they can be accommodated in the same geographical area on the same day. She doesn't subscribe to the notion that one job a day is enough, and she hates wasted effort.

As with all successful Private Secretaries, Peter Gibbs has a certain amount of influence with his boss. He knows the best way to present a case to her and also when and how to draw attention to a particular letter if he feels it is worthwhile. But the final decisions are always hers, and once she has decided it is very difficult to get her to change her mind.

There are certain 'fixed feasts' around which the programme has to be planned each year. School holidays are sacrosanct, so would-be hosts are advised not to try for August, Easter or around Christmas. The third Monday in June is also out as this is when the annual service of the Order of the Garter is held. Once the draft programme has been decided, Peter Gibbs tells the Ladies-in-Waiting, so that they can decide between themselves who is going to do which particular engagement. Then Philip Robinson, head of the Princess's security force, is informed, so that he can allocate one of the four bodyguards.

Where the Ladies-in-Waiting are concerned, the Princess mainly leaves the arrangements to them. She has no favourites and doesn't mind which of them goes where. She is all too aware of their family commitments (only one of them, Victoria Legge-Bourke, is single) and she also realizes that they have other, outside responsibilities. One runs an art gallery, another is a magistrate, a third owns and operates a large country estate, one lives most of the time in Scotland, while yet another is married to a senior Army officer and has duties associated with his regiment. None of them is employed full-time, and as most of them live outside London, it makes good sense to have a rota that does not involve too much unnecessary travel. Lady Carew-Pole lives in Cornwall, so obviously any engagements in the West Country would be convenient for her. Shân Legge-Bourke has special connections in Wales, so she tends to look after things in that part of the United Kingdom. Jane Holderness-Roddam and Caroline Nunneley specialize in equestrian engagements, and Rowena Feilden and Victoria Legge-Bourke are usually available in London or the Home Counties. It's a system that seems to work very well and the only time there might be a slight difference of opinion is when a particularly attractive overseas tour comes up. There's often quite a bit of competition for these trips, even the ones to outlandish places like Upper Volta (now Burkina Faso) where living conditions, even for Royals and their staff, are sometimes less comfortable than they have been used to.

Occasionally Buckingham Palace receives enquiries from women asking how one becomes a Lady-in-Waiting. It's a good question, to which there is no single answer. Each female member of the Royal Family has different methods of choosing these companions and if ever the post were to be advertised, a job description might appear as follows:

Wanted, ladies of good character, well born with perfect manners, to accompany ladies of the Royal Family on engagements at home and abroad. Titles are not necessary but an advantage, and the ability to hold intelligent conversations with anyone from a dustman to a duke is of prime importance. Good mixers, with accommodating families as much time is spent away from home, and great physical stamina as hours are spent standing at receptions and cocktail parties. A good sense of humour is essential as is the ability to maintain an appearance of interest when confronted by boring politicians and civic dignitaries at Palace functions. There is no salary, but out-of-pocket expenses will be reimbursed, plus a small dress allowance if required. Long, irregular hours, no paid holidays, but extensive first-class travel—and a social cachet second to none.

One of the ladies suggested that one other qualification might be added—'a cast-iron bladder'.

Unfortunately, neither this nor any other similar advertisement is ever likely to appear in the newspapers or the fashionable magazines read by possible candidates. The Ladies-in-Waiting to the Queen, the Queen Mother, the Princess Royal and all the other ladies in the Royal Family are all chosen by personal invitation only. You cannot apply, you have to wait to be asked. And as most of them carry on well into old age, it is also usually a case of filling a dead woman's shoes.

The Queen's fourteen Ladies-in-Waiting fall into different categories, led by the Mistress of the Robes, the senior Lady who is always a Duchess.

180

Then there are Ladies of the Bedchamber, not to be confused with the next level, Women of the Bedchamber, who work a rota system of two weeks on/two weeks off. If things get really hectic, there are also Extra Ladies and Extra Women of the Bedchamber to help out.

The Princess Royal has ten Ladies-in-Waiting, including three Extras. The most senior in years of service is Lady (Mary) Carew-Pole who was the first to be appointed back in 1970. She was not a personal friend of the Princess at the time, but she did become involved through the old-girl network as she had two good friends who were then Ladies-in-Waiting to the Queen. She received her invitation to join Princess Anne's household through a third party, Lady Euston (now the Duchess of Grafton, the Mistress of the Robes). This is the way in which nearly all Ladies-in-Waiting are recruited. There is rarely a direct approach from the prospective Royal employer, so if someone wants to decline the offer—which has never happened in living memory—there is no possibility of a snub.

Within a few months of Lady Carew-Pole (she was Mary Dawnay in those days) arriving at the Palace, she was joined by the second Lady-in-Waiting, Rowena Brassey (now Mrs Feilden), who had some previous experience as she had been performing the same role for more than two years for the wife of the Governor-General of New Zealand. In fact it was during Princess Anne's visit to that country that they first met. Rowena Feilden says that when she started it was a full-time job as there were only three people in the Household. 'I certainly considered myself to be an employee and regarded the money I received as salary as I had no other job.'

It was after the Princess's first marriage in 1973 that the number of public engagements started to multiply rapidly and the office expanded. Victoria Legge-Bourke had been a fellow pupil of the Princess at Benenden, though as she puts it, 'I was a year ahead of her so our paths didn't really cross all that much. We were never close friends.' Victoria had the perfect pedigree to become a Royal Aide. Her brother had been a Page of Honour to the Queen, she knew many people in the Royal Household, and she had, as a teenager, once been invited to join a small skiing party at Val d'Isère in France where the Princess was also a guest. Another guest at the same party was Leonora, the Countess of Lichfield, who was also to become a Lady-in-Waiting at a later date.

Once Victoria was established, she suggested that a fourth Lady-in-Waiting should be invited to join them. Her name is Celia Innes, an elegant, friendly and outgoing woman of immense charm who combines her Royal duties with running a successful florist's business in London. Married, with two children, she found herself invited to a party at Windsor Castle without, she says, 'the faintest idea why'. Having passed the first hurdle without even knowing that she was being tested, she was then asked to several more functions, and finally Victoria Legge-Bourke asked her if she would like to consider becoming 'one of them'. Before agreeing, she wrote to the Princess explaining about her other commitments, family and business, 'Did the Princess mind coming third in the order of priorities?' It must have been quite a shock to Princess Anne at the time to be put in her place so strongly, but she has always preferred people to speak their mind, and she agreed that she was perfectly willing to accept the situation. Celia has been with her ever since, even though these days her role has been reduced, at her own request, to that of an Extra.

When Shân Legge-Bourke joined the Household it was assumed, wrongly, that this was through the influence of her sister-in-law, Victoria. In fact, the person who suggested her name to the Princess was Celia Innes. Shân has probably got the biggest outside commitments of all the Ladies as she inherited an enormous country estate in Wales from her father, Lord Glanusk. Although she employs an estate manager, she is very much a hands-on landlord and almost every day can be found on some part of the estate, checking that the work she has ordered to be carried out has been done to her satisfaction. She is also involved in a number of public duties in her own right, including being Chief Commissioner for Wales of the St John Ambulance Cadets. Once a year she opens Glanusk Park to the cadets for their annual camp where she is very much in evidence wearing her distinctive sweatshirt with the giant letters C.O.W. (Commissioner of Wales) emblazoned across her chest.

Araminta Ritchie is the wife of a senior Army officer who has served in Northern Ireland in one of the most delicate positions. So much so, that in the book which is issued to all members of the Royal Household listing the names, telephone numbers and private addresses of all members of the Royal Family and their staff, and known as 'The

183

Green Book', she is listed as being contactable only through the Buckingham Palace switchboard. She now lives in Paris where her husband is based but she still manages to commute to London regularly when she is required for Royal duties.

Caroline Nunneley is the Lady-in-Waiting who has known the Princess longer than almost anyone else in the Household. As we saw in Chapter 9, she used to be a groom at Alison Oliver's stables when the Princess started her serious riding. Once married to Malcolm Wallace, now of the Jockey Club, but formerly Director of the British Equestrian Association, Caroline is now Mrs William Nunneley. She is a professional sculptress with a foundry in Swindon from where she sells her work all over the world and obviously she shares a common interest in matters equestrian with her Royal boss.

The only other Lady who was approached personally by the Princess Royal is Jane Holderness-Roddam (formerly Jane Bullen), twice winner at Badminton (1968 and 1978), and Olympic rider at the Mexico Games in 1968. No one has more credentials than she as a companion to the former European Champion, and her invitation to join the Princess Royal came by way of a telephone call. She told me she was called one Friday afternoon by the Princess and asked if she would care to join the team. 'The Princess told me to think about it over the weekend and maybe talk to one or two of the others to find out what was required. I knew her well as a competitor,' she remembers, 'but you never get to know someone like her very closely. I was very flattered to be asked, of course, but I was glad she gave me some time to think about it as I had no idea what being a Lady-in-Waiting involved. Fortunately I knew Shân Legge-Bourke, so I spoke to her about it and she explained how the system worked. The following Monday I telephoned the Princess and said I would be delighted and honoured to accept.'

In the early days Jane encountered a few problems, such as the day she found out in a positive fashion that the Princess does not care to have anyone touch her things. 'I once moved some papers of hers thinking I was helping, only to be told in no uncertain terms that "the papers are left that way because that's the way I want them left". I never moved anything of hers ever again. I also learned how to recognize the signs when she wanted to be left alone—or when she wanted to talk. She's very easy to work for and very considerate. If she hears that one of us has been ill or had some family mishap, she will always ring up herself to see if she can do anything to help, or send flowers.'

The most recent of the Ladies is Mrs David Bowes-Lyon, whose husband is related to the Strathmores, the family of Queen Elizabeth the Queen Mother. Harriet Bowes-Lyon, whose home is in Scotland, also has impeccable credentials, as her mother, The Lady Margaret Colville, CVO, has been a Lady-in-Waiting to the Queen Mother for some years. As many of the Princess's engagements take place north of the border, it is convenient to have someone familiar with the area and who lives locally, to act as companion and assistant.

The Ladies-in-Waiting are not all out of the same mould, though they do tend to know many of the same people. Victoria Legge-Bourke is the only one with an Oxbridge education. When it was revealed that she had won a place at Oxford University from Benenden, it was such a rare occurrence that the school was given a half-day holiday to celebrate. Victoria is a tall, blonde chain-smoker, very gregarious, who gets on with everybody. Her sister-in-law, Shân, is practical, tough (and a dedicated non-smoker) who thrives in the hardest conditions. She likes few things more than accompanying the Princess Royal to remote African villages where the local idea of a shower is a bucket of cold water behind a makeshift curtain.

Lady Carew-Pole is slightly older than the others and possibly the sort of person one could imagine becoming a Mistress of the Robes one day. Jane Holderness-Roddam is small, compact, superbly fit, and physically not unlike the Olympic ice-skating star, Jayne Torvill. As one of the world's most successful horsewomen, she has had her share of falls, and when you see her in her role as Royal associate, it is sometimes difficult to imagine her controlling several tons of horseflesh.

Celia Innes is delightful: always smiling, rarely seen in a bad mood, and someone who finds no hardship in talking to young, inexperienced, tongue-tied teenagers or boring old civic dignitaries with vastly inflated ideas of their own importance. She reckons the Princess's sense of humour is a safety valve, 'She has the greatest sense of fun and some of her comments, particularly when we are driving slowly through a crowd, and she can hear what they are saying about her, should be written down for posterity.' Of course, they never are. None of the Ladies would dream of publishing anything they learn from, or about, the Royal

Family, which in some ways is a pity as it might show a more human side to the public face.

The Princess also recognizes the need for a sense of humour in her Ladies, saying, 'It's no good at all if you get someone turning up in the morning looking like death, and furious and ratty about life and uncommunicative . . . What they have to be is good at chatting to people and making them feel comfortable, because that helps me . . . so if, when they go out on a job, they just stand in a corner looking glum and bored, that's no help to anyone, least of all the people at the other end, never mind to me. So it's important that they should be capable of being interested and mixing with the people we meet.'

Rowena Feilden is the quietest of the Ladies but that doesn't mean she lets the others get away with anything. Her term as a Lady-in-Waiting stretches back twenty-five years and having shared with the 'boss' one of the most traumatic experiences when the kidnap attempt was made in 1974 (see Chapter 4), she occupies a special place which no one else can ever usurp.

The one thing common to all the Ladies-in-Waiting is their complete loyalty to the Princess Royal. They recognize that she has her faults, but while they may discuss them among themselves they would never talk about her to outsiders. She attracts respect and admiration for her dedication to her work, and as Lady Carew-Pole has said, 'We all take it in turns to be on duty. She is there all the time and often we are the ones who flag while she keeps on going. Her energy is tremendous and her enthusiasm is catching. She never gives the impression of being bored or tired.'

187

The nearest any of them has come to commenting on the feelings of the Princess is perhaps Shân Legge-Bourke's defence of her when she was accused of being unfeeling in the press. 'Of course she cares about people. She is one of the most compassionate of women. It's just that she doesn't wear her heart on her sleeve, so it's sometimes difficult to know exactly what she's feeling.'

Chief Inspector Philip Robinson is unique among Royal policemen in that he has spent his entire time at Buckingham Palace guarding the Princess Royal. Every other officer in the Royal and Diplomatic Protection Department has been moved around, looking after different members of the family, but Robinson started with the young Princess Anne and has remained with her ever since. The feeling at Buckingham Palace is that he will probably stay where he is until he retires. Tall and slim, with iron-grey hair fashionably cut and always immaculately dressed, Philip Robinson looks the part of the Royal bodyguard as most people imagine it. An expert in unarmed combat, he would not hesitate to hit anyone he even suspected of trying to harm the Princess, without a second thought. Like all his colleagues, he never leaves Gatcombe or the Palace without checking to see that his gun is working and is easily accessible. Even when he appears in full morning dress at formal functions, his weapon is neatly tucked away, and had he been on duty in The Mall when the attempted kidnapping took place, one gets the feeling that he would have shot first and asked questions later.

Philip Robinson supervises the small security

team that guards the Princess round the clock, allocating their duties and making sure they all attend the refresher courses that are constantly held to keep them up to date with the latest anti-terrorist and general security developments. The Princess has four police officers working for her, including one woman, but contrary to what most people imagine, they are not detectives, but uniformed police officers from the Metropolitan Force who happen to carry out their duties in plain clothes. Nor are they Members of the Royal Household. They are part of Scotland Yard's Specialist Operations Department, which pays their salaries and all their expenses. So when the Princess—or the Queen for that matter—travels abroad on an official trip, with the Foreign Office or some other organization paying their expenses, all the costs of transport and subsistence for the accompanying police officers are met by the Metropolitan Police, their parent force. The officers are never allowed to accept 'freebies' either. If the Princess has been given a free ride by an airline, which would also be delighted to offer the same facility to those travelling with her, the policeman has to refuse. Everything is done strictly by the book.

The police officers work an eight-day shift system, beginning on Friday when they report at Gatcombe to relieve whoever is on duty. If the Princess is working in the house or riding on the estate, they do not accompany her as she is regarded as being on 'secure premises'. The same applies at Buckingham Palace. So during such times the policeman will remain in his room, perhaps filling out his expenses or studying for a promotion examination. The officers take all the usual exams but unless they leave the Palace and return to mainstream policing, they can find promotion slow. At Gatcombe they eat in the kitchen with the rest of the staff, and whenever the Princess leaves the estate, her bodyguard goes with her. He would never permit her to go out unaccompanied even if she wanted to. But she knows the rules and does not try to make life any more difficult than it already is. Her attitude to her police detail is one of resigned tolerance. She knows they have a job to do and, while it may irritate her at times, puts up with it, knowing that the alternative could be a thousand times worse.

Theoretically the police officers' routine is well planned and should give them three weeks off once their eight-day stint is finished. In practice, it rarely works out so well. One of them may often be away with Peter Gibbs, carrying out a recce for a future royal visit, while another might be at Hereford on a course with the SAS, with the usual leave entitlements being taken as well. So the system has to involve a certain amount of give and take.

The Princess knows how disruptive to normal family life working for her can be and she is sympathetic to the problems of her staff, so she tries to make up for it by making sure spouses get invited to Royal functions such as Garden Parties and Christmas lunches. Even so, marriages can come under tremendous strain and break up. Philip Robinson's was one such casualty. He was divorced some years ago but was happily remarried in 1996 to a young Spanish woman he met during the Barcelona Olympic Games, when his boss was present as a member of the International Olympic

Committee.

The police officer occupies a unique position among Royal Aides. He is not employed by the Queen or any other member of the Royal Family, yet he spends more time with them than any fully fledged Member of the Royal Household. He is frequently alone with his Royal charge for hours on end when they are driving to and from an engagement and, as such, he has to be particularly careful not to get too familiar. It is a trap several policemen in the past have fallen into—and just as quickly they have found themselves removed from all Royal duties and back working in some suburban London police station.

One officer tried to sell his story to the newspapers, claiming he was having an affair with the Princess and that she had been chasing after him for months. Rumours had circulated for some time about Anne and one of her minders being too close, and when the officer's superiors got to hear of it he was quickly relieved of his post.

Another bodyguard who couldn't keep his mouth shut about his Royal boss was quietly shunted aside. He claimed the Princess used to make personal remarks about him in front of others. He was rather sensitive about his receding hairline and on one occasion the Princess said to him, 'It's enough to make your hair curl—or it would be if you had any.' He didn't understand that to work for the Princess Royal you sometimes need a thick skin.

Philip Robinson has known Peter and Zara Phillips since they were infants, and when they were very young he and his colleagues were often photographed strolling around Badminton or some other venue holding the hand of one of the children or carrying them on their shoulders. It gave the impression that the policemen were 'Uncle' figures who were part of the family. Robinson says it was a false picture as he and his fellow officers were merely carrying out their duty. There was no personal relationship, 'We were just part of the furniture. If we moved on tomorrow, the children knew that someone else would be there to take our places.'

There are few perks to being a Royal protection officer. There is no extra pay apart from a clothing allowance to pay for the suits, tropical wear, dinner jackets and formal morning coats that are required on various occasions. The ability to blend in with the surroundings is all-important, and certainly some officers do not mind giving the impression that they are James Bond figures. Being a Royal bodyguard is undoubtedly one of the most glamorous postings any policeman can get. They are all volunteers, and for every one who is selected, a further twenty are turned down.

Their relationship with the rest of the Household is delicate. A police officer earns much more than the Household staff. A Chief Inspector gets over £34,000 a year, while even Sergeants—who make up the bulk of the Royal Protection Department—earn over £25,000. There are very few in the Royal Household who come anywhere near making this sort of money.

Officially, Peter Gibbs is head of the Princess Royal's Household and all the others take their orders from him. But he is not Philip Robinson's boss, so even though they work very closely together, Lieutenant Colonel Gibbs's requirements are made to Chief Inspector Robinson in the form of requests rather than orders.

When an invitation to the Princess Royal has been accepted, the administrative machinery is set in motion. The date and time and draft programme are agreed, and then a recce visit is carried out by one of the police officers who will go over every step of the proposed visit, finding out who the Princess will meet, and how many dignitaries expect to be presented. If, say, a plaque is to be unveiled, the wording has to be agreed and a number of rehearsals held to see that the curtain covering the plaque moves smoothly.

If a meal is planned, the menu is carefully vetted. The Princess is not fussy about food but hosts are advised that shellfish should never be included, and as she does not like hanging about, an hour is considered long enough for lunch. Although she does not smoke herself, she has no objection to others doing so in her presence, but she should not be offered wine as she never drinks any alcohol. Instead, fresh orange juice or mineral water should be available.

Speeches are to be kept to an absolute minimum, and if a gift is to be offered it should not be too expensive or ostentatious. The Private Secretary must be told in advance what the gift is and its value—the Princess hates surprises. If she is expected to sign the visitors' book, a fresh page should be kept for her signature alone, and if a chairman's granddaughter is to present a bouquet of flowers, it should be small and unwired. Too many Royal hands have been snagged on wired bunches of flowers, resulting in their being unable to shake hands for the rest of the day.

193

If the Princess is arriving by car, hosts are told that she will be sitting in the seat immediately behind the chauffeur, unless she is driving herself, which she frequently does. Not one of her police officers has ever been given the opportunity of driving her.

The location of lavatories is noted, with the request that one should be kept for the Princess's exclusive use. Shân Legge-Bourke has on more than one occasion kept the Princess in the loo for several minutes when hosts have needed a little more time to get themselves organized.

If the Princess is attending a church service, officials are told that it is perfectly all right to offer her the collection plate. Her Private Secretary or policeman actually carries the money and hands it to her.

Hosts are often confused about how to address her. The answer is, when first being presented she is called Your Royal Highness, with a neck-bow from men and a curtsy from women, and subsequently the form of address is Ma'am (with a short A to rhyme with 'ham', not the longer A as in 'smarm').

The media requirements will be discussed. The Princess does not like cameramen and reporters to be too intrusive or to be placed where they might interfere with the people she has come to meet. At the same time they have to be given positions where they can observe what is going on, and in the provinces she does not like the idea of the regional press being overshadowed by their counterparts from the nationals. So requirements and egos have to be delicately balanced.

The police officer will have his own priorities.

He checks all the buildings along the proposed route, looking at the security aspect, and liaises with his opposite numbers in the local police force. This is when he has to use all his diplomatic skills as he is frequently dealing with officers of superior rank, but who have to defer to him in matters relating to Royalty.

Once the recce is complete, a final programme is produced. One of the characteristics that marks a successful Private Secretary is his attention to detail. In the fourteen years that Peter Gibbs has been running the Princess Royal's office he has established an enviable reputation in an organization that prides itself on leaving no 't' uncrossed and no 'i' undotted. He says that after thirty years in the Army this has become second nature. Whatever the reason, the Princess Royal's office is regarded as one of the most efficient—and cost-effective—in Buckingham Palace.

The Princess prides herself on being thrifty and this is passed on to her staff. For the twelve-day visit to Atlanta, Georgia, for the 1996 Olympic Games, it was decided that it would be uneconomical to take the usual team of Private Secretary, Lady-in-Waiting, personal dresser and one of the lady clerks. Instead the Princess, whose expenses were being met by the International Olympic Committee, of which she is a member, was accompanied only by Maddy Louloudis, who acted as Lady-in-Waiting, Private Secretary and dresser, all in one. The police officer, as usual, had his expenses, air fare and hotel paid for by the Metropolitan Police.

The back-up team work long hours for comparatively modest pay and few perks. The only obvious advantage is being able to park for nothing in front of the best address in the capital and the chance to have ringside seats at some of the finest Royal ceremonials. There may also be the hidden thought that if they want to leave Royal service for more lucrative employment, a good reference written on Buckingham Palace headed paper opens a lot of doors.

The team are all loyal to their boss and reckon that no matter how hard they have to work, she works harder than any of them. Perhaps that is the main reason why they stay for years on end when in many of the other Households at the Palace, turnover of staff occurs with monotonous regularity. The Princess, in turn, is highly appreciative of her staff's efforts, and though she could never be described as a woman who gushes, they all know that their work does not go unnoticed.

Once a year, in the week before Christmas, the Princess Royal invites all her staff to a special lunch in Gloucestershire. At one time it was held at Gatcombe, but as the domestic staff based there lost out because they had to be on duty, they now all go to nearby Chavenage House, just over the hill from Gatcombe, where everybody can join in the fun.

Chavenage is a delightful sixteenth-century manor house with the reputation of being one of the most haunted houses in England; there is an Oliver Cromwell room said to be inhabited by several ghosts of Civil War vintage. It is owned by David Lowsley-Williams, a former Army officer, who employs outside caterers when a large function is being planned. Referring to the Princess

Royal's Christmas lunch party, he says it is one of the happiest and most informal occasions of the year. 'Everybody dresses in their best, all the guests are allowed to bring their partners, so it's quite a large group, around fifty or so. Mark always comes, with his farm workers, and Peter and Zara usually turn up, but Tim Laurence hasn't been so far.' The menu is traditional Christmas fare; there's plenty of drink and lots of laughter. The house is decorated, the tree is dressed and there's a truly festive spirit all around. It makes a splendid start to the holiday season. Everybody gets a chance to talk to the Princess and her family, and as David Lowsley-Williams explained, 'There's no stiffness between Mark and Her Royal Highness. It's just like any other normal family party.' The Princess gives out her Christmas presents (the value of the gifts is not great, and there's no chance of cashmere sweaters, which is what the Princess of Wales used to give her staff occasionally).

By making use of modern technology the Princess manages to keep her team compact and tightly controlled. She does not even make use of an Equerry, although she is entitled to one as she is associated with several military and naval units. It is just that she and her Private Secretary believe that 'small is beautiful' where the office is concerned, and an extra body would be not only unnecessary but a nuisance.

Elsewhere in the Palace, management consultants have been brought in to try to streamline (in other words cut down) the Royal Household. They would have a difficult job in finding areas in the Princess Royal's office where they could reduce the costs. But if they were successful in showing her how to save even more money, she would be the first to thank them and to adopt their measures.

The Princess Royal hates waste and loves the idea of getting a bargain. So when she decided she wanted one of the best motorcars in the world—a Bentley Turbo—she shied away from paying over £100,000 in one go. Instead, after consulting financial experts, she opted for the easier and far less painful method of contract hire. This means she now pays around £2,000 a month for the car, but it comes with full maintenance, including tyres (which at £125 each can be an expensive item with the high mileage she does each year). And if the car has to be off the road for any reason, she gets a replacement vehicle immediately. That is the sort of efficiency that appeals to her thrifty nature. Whether she is spending her own or other people's money, the Princess Royal is an expert in demanding and getting full value.

CHAPTER THIRTEEN

THE PRINCESS AND THE PRESS

The Princess Royal is alone among the Royal Family in that her attitude to the Press has never changed. Every one of the others, including the Queen herself, has at some time found it necessary, or at least convenient, to accommodate members of the Fourth Estate when they have needed favourable coverage. Not Anne; she has always regarded the media as an unnecessary evil and one which she would happily do without at all times.

In fact, one of the few things that really upsets the Princess is the Press themselves. 'The questions they ask me are almost always meaningless,' she complains. 'If I've spent the day in a place where children are dying of starvation and disease, they will ask me what I had for breakfast.' The fact that she is unable or unwilling to substantiate this claim, or list a single instance when such an exchange took place, gives rise to the thought that perhaps she is simply using this extreme example of unprofessionalism as a generalization to attack a group for which she obviously has little time.

While it is perfectly true that in the past the media have had little love for her either, it is patently untrue that they never report her words or actions accurately. In the early days of her public life her usually sullen attitude was reflected in the way reporters and photographers treated her, unfavourably. She replaced her aunt Princess Margaret as the Royal the Press loved to hate and she alternated with her father, Prince Philip, as the person they chose to attack. But in the last eight or ten years she has been given a mainly favourable press and her work for the Save the Children Fund has placed her in a position that is a cross between that of Mother Theresa and Albert Schweitzer, so any newspaper or magazine that wrote disparagingly about her would do so at the risk of upsetting many of its readers.

One of her main complaints about the treatment she gets is that the substance of her message never seems to get across, because, she says, if there's no scandal attached then the Press is simply not interested. In her own words, 'The knockers just have to have someone.'

One occasion when she didn't object to a 'minor scandal' story was at the 1984 Olympic Games in Los Angeles. The British super-athlete, Daley Thompson, won the gold medal in the Decathlon, becoming champion of champions, and there to congratulate him was Anne, in her capacity as President of the British Olympic Association. They hit it off immediately, each recognizing in the other the same singlemindedness, dedication and determination it takes to become a world-beater.

After the medal presentation ceremony Thompson and the Princess joked together and obviously enjoyed each other's company. At the Press conference that followed Daley was asked what they had talked about. His reply that they discussed 'making babies together' made headlines the next day, with the Press supposedly scandalized at the implied insult. The Princess, however, was the first to see the joke and she took it in great part, saying, 'The Press always ask people to whom I speak what we were talking about, and people have different ways of contriving not to tell them. This was the way Daley Thompson chose.'

This was one occasion when Anne was able to beat the Press at their own game, but generally she objects to the way in which she is usually presented to the reading public as a person of tetchy unfriendliness. This is the result of her natural wariness with reporters and the fact that she has never become overfriendly with any of them. There are no favoured few among Fleet Street's Royal rat-pack, so they, or at least some of them, have retaliated by interpreting her reserve as arrogance, and her natural suspicion as haughtiness. James

Whitaker, the doyen of Royal reporters in Britain, sums up perfectly the difference in the treatment that two Princesses might receive. 'If both Diana, Princess of Wales and the Princess Royal were competing at a horse show, the photographers would all be waiting at the finish to see Diana get her trophy, and at the water jump to see Anne fall in—that's the difference.'

The Princess rarely unbends towards members of the Fourth Estate, and one who has more cause then most to resent her attitude—although she doesn't—is Jayne Fincher, one of the world's most successful photographers of Royalty, and also one of the nicest. Jayne, who has followed the Princess faithfully for many years on practically every overseas tour, including several where she has been the only member of the Press Corps present, has still to receive her first acknowledgement by the Princess. They have travelled thousands of miles together, or at least with Jayne trailing along behind the official party, and not once has she ever had even a 'Good morning' from Her Royal Highness.

Jayne Fincher knows that she hasn't been ignored on personal grounds, even though the Princess is always aware when she is present, it's just that Anne believes there is no earthly reason why she should have anything to do with the Press, in spite of the fact that for more than ten years they have almost invariably written nice things about her and her work. Jayne still regards the Princess Royal as the most interesting member of the Royal Family and says, 'I like covering Princess Anne's trips because they're interesting and relatively informal.' Her loyalty to the Princess also paid off handsomely when she managed to get the first photograph of Anne and Tim together. 'I was due to cover the Caledonian Ball, which Anne attends, but I didn't really want to go. My mum said to me, "Oh, you never know you might get Tim and Anne dancing." When I got there they turned up together and I was absolutely amazed. I thought, "There's going to be a terrible scene if I take a photo," but I finally plucked up enough courage and walked straight up to them. I stood there and it was obvious—because Princess Anne will soon tell you if she doesn't want something—that she didn't mind. So I started taking pictures. She was smiling away and it was the first time I'd really seen her looking happy. It was a terrific scoop.'

It hasn't been easy for the Princess Royal to see a young woman, not of Royal birth, come into the family and take over as the star, eclipsing every other member without, apparently, any effort on her own part. While Anne would visit Northern Ireland at the height of the Troubles to see for herself the privations the soldiers and their families were suffering, Diana would attend a glamorous dinner in London, and scoop all the headlines and photographs. Diana's picture appeared in every newspaper above captions that read, 'Dazzling Di' or 'The Crown Jewel' with columns devoted to every detail of her dress, hair, make-up and diamonds. For news of Anne's visit one had to turn to the Court Circular, issued by the Buckingham Palace Press Office, with the bare announcement that she had visited Northern Ireland. In other words, it was a complete non-event in news terms and so far as editors and their readers were concerned, might never have happened.

While the Princess Royal has never actively courted the Press, she is concerned about the way people see her, and those closest to her say her tough exterior has been deliberately developed as a protective shield behind which to hide. She is a realist, however, and she knows full well the impact that some of her more controversial public statements have made. When she described AIDS as a 'self-inflicted wound' the Press leaped on the story, which they saw as revealing for the first time what a member of the Royal Family felt about homosexuals. Several editorials supported her, writing of her as a champion of family values and heterosexual (in other words, normal) relationships.

Although the Princess never intended her words to be used for this purpose, she was aware of what she was saying and of the impact the phrase would have. Nevertheless, one of her main complaints against the Press is the way in which she feels that what she says is taken out of context. 'There are certain people who embroider some of the things I say to make them sound controversial. If only they would report exactly what I had said—in the proper context—without adding their own interpretation, there would be no controversy.'

One occasion, however, when her own words, reported verbatim, did cause controversy was at a conference of the Victim Support Group in Glasgow early in 1996. The Princess accused the experts in post-traumatic distress of inventing the illness for their own ends. In fact, she suggested that the fashionable diagnosis of post-traumatic stress disorder itself might well be simply an invention. Casting doubts on the mini-industry that has grown up around recent disasters such as the Pan-American Lockerbie bomb atrocity, she said, 'The tendency is, the more information you gather, the more likely you are to stick a certain label on certain attitudes, which I suspect is where post-traumatic stress came from ... It was a convenient lumping together of the results of particular situations ... Professionals have always been prone to hijacking the subject once they have invented it.'

It was an explosive statement and attracted a predictable reaction from the very professionals she was attacking. Several eminent psychologists made disparaging comments about the Princess's 'lack of medical qualifications' and suggested she would do better to 'maintain her silence'. What they had not acknowledged was that she was speaking from the victim's point of view. As someone who had been through one of the most traumatic experiences of all—an attempted kidnapping by an armed madman—she was all too aware of what post-traumatic stress should be. After being a target herself in 1974 neither she, her then husband, nor her Lady-in-Waiting, was offered any counselling, and there do not appear to have been any serious after-effects.

The Press, and not only the tabloids, had a field-day following the speech. The Princess Royal's words were reported prominently, and accurately, on the front pages of several broadsheet newspapers, and once again she had been responsible for starting a public debate on a subject many people were afraid of raising.

Nobody could ever accuse her of not having the courage of her convictions, or of hiding behind anonymity when she turns on her attackers. In the days when the television personality Robert Kilroy-Silk also had a weekly newspaper column, he wrote an article criticizing Anne's views on BSE (Mad Cow Disease)—this was before the most recent Euro-row on the subject in 1996. She had publicly stated that she felt beef was still safe to eat. In reply she said, 'I do know some things, strange as it may seem to Mr Kilroy-Silk. When I spoke out on BSE . . . I had already received the information which I felt gave me the right to form an opinion.'

Yet again the Princess Royal had spoken out on the kind of controversial subject in which some people feel the Royal Family should not become involved. She disagrees, 'Nonsense! When does a commonly discussed subject become controversial? Anyway, members of the Family have often spoken out on matters of national and international interest. Why shouldn't they? It's just bad luck if you open your mouth about a subject which just happens to become of interest to the media.'

In the early days of her public career Anne earned the reputation of being 'Princess Sourpuss' or, as the *Daily Mirror* called her, 'The Frown Princess' because she constantly refused to do what the other Royals had always done, that is, cooperate with reporters and photographers. Queen Elizabeth the Queen Mother is the darling of the media. She can do no wrong in their eyes. She invariably knows the right angle to show herself to her best advantage and she always pauses long enough to allow photographers to get their pictures. On one occasion she even waited while an unfortunate photographer changed cameras after one had jammed, saying, 'Are you sure you've got it now?'

The Princess Royal would never do that. In fact, on more than one occasion she has been known to turn away deliberately so that photographers are unable to get a decent shot. She made her feelings about Press photographers very plain when she replied to one who had expressed the hope that he was not being a pest, by saying, 'You are a pest, by the very nature of that camera in your hand.' This was in 1972 at the Burghley Horse Trials when she was just twenty-two and was only three or four years into her career in public life, so it did not augur well for the future that she was being so openly confrontational. The libraries of all the tabloid newspapers in Britain are filled with cuttings cataloguing what they regard as the Princess Royal's failings, mainly, it has to be admitted, because of her attitude when she has been accosted on the riding field. Her profanities— a normal part of equestrian life—made brilliant headlines for over a decade, written by journalists who professed to be shocked to hear four-letter words on the lips of the Queen's only daughter.

In 1991, in an effort to put the record straight, the Princess Royal, aided by the racing journalist Ivor Herbert, wrote her own account of her life. It was not an autobiography in the accepted sense, in that many of the most interesting facts were omitted altogether or dismissed in a sentence or two: for example, her first marriage was covered in three lines which said, 'I was to make the transition from being a carefree spinster living at home to a careworn wife looking after her own home . . .'. But the book does give in minute detail the Princess's attitude to horses and her involvement with them since childhood, and of course its accuracy cannot be faulted. Andrew Parker Bowles recalls seeing her several times at Gatcombe 'tapping away at her word-processor'. So no one can accuse her of not having written the book herself.

On overseas tours, particularly those involving the Save the Children Fund, when there are often marvellous photo-opportunities, the Princess still refuses to cooperate. A former Director-General of the Fund, Nicholas Hinton, used to despair of his Royal President when he had gone to enormous trouble setting up suitable pictures. She would simply ignore the photographers and he would then have the task of trying to explain to the irate group why she wouldn't be filmed holding a starving baby—a picture that would certainly have made the national newspapers back home and might have helped the visual impact of the Fund. It wouldn't have done her image any harm either.

These days the Princess has lost her reputation as a truculent and sometimes offensive young woman and has been transformed into the 'Caring Princess' who will do anything and go anywhere so long as one of her charities benefits. She still doesn't 'do stunts' but her practical approach to her job and her no-nonsense attitude, especially when she is out in the field, have allowed her to overcome the initial dislike the Press felt for her. She says she has never changed—'it's other people's perception of me that's changed'—and that her alleged non-cooperation with the media is simply her refusal to be manipulated. Others say it is just another manifestation of her independence of spirit, a characteristic inherited from her father, the Duke of Edinburgh, who has also been known to say exactly what he thinks. As far back as 1954, he was heard to remark, 'God save us from those bloody vultures', referring to a group of Press photographers during a Royal tour of the Pacific.

One thing is certain, the Princess is now taken seriously in everything she says and cannot complain these days of not being reported accurately. While the tabloids would still love to print a scandal about her if they could find one, they now realize that she is more likely to produce newsworthy stories of a serious nature as she travels the world as a roving ambassadress.

One of the most recent occasions when she made news, however, was over something she could well have done without. A man had been stalking her for many months, appearing at most of her public engagements, so much so that she drew the attention of the security officers to him. He was eventually arrested, and subsequently charged with a breach of the peace offence, but was discharged—even though he had admitted writing to the Queen about the Princess and also saying that he had had sexual fantasies about her. The court decided there was no case to answer, however. The incident attracted headlines for several days, with every account being sympathetic to the Princess Royal. Such attention by a man is unwelcome to any woman, be it film star, Princess or the average woman in the street. There can be few things more frightening than to know someone is following your every movement, even if later the courts in their wisdom decide that he intended no harm. The Press coverage on this occasion helped to bring the man to the attention of the authorities, and at least his pestering stopped after his arrest.

Where radio and television are concerned the

Princess handles herself brilliantly. She knows exactly what she wants to say, and as someone who has accumulated a fair amount of experience over the past twenty-five years, she also knows how to fit into the time constraints the media impose. She has given major interviews to Michael Parkinson (in Australia with Mark Phillips when Parkinson had to pay £6,000 to the Save the Children Fund) and to Terry Wogan, on prime-time British television, when the repartee was so sparkling it was said that it must have been rehearsed and scripted (it wasn't). She later told me that she enjoyed Wogan because of his wit and good humour and the fact that she was never quite sure what he was going to say next. She liked the challenge.

The Princess was also interviewed by the political commentator Brian Walden, on ITV, but with less success (she had been looking forward to a tougher confrontation), and there have been innumerable shorter radio and television interviews either before or after one of her overseas tours. One television programme which left her slightly dissatisfied was when she agreed to talk to Terry Waite (before he was taken hostage in Beirut). Afterwards she said she wished their positions had been reversed and she could have asked the questions.

I myself was involved closely with the Princess's most extended television programme when Thames Television followed her for a whole year filming her life and work. We had no restrictions placed on us, apart from the occasional switching off by her of a radio microphone that we had secreted in her handbag, and which she sometimes felt was a little too intrusive. She was totally professional towards the camera crew and voluntarily relinquished all editorial control over the finished product. In spite of her cooperation she was betrayed by one of our group who sold his inside story of what life was like at Gatcombe and Buckingham Palace to a Sunday tabloid newspaper. She was understandably furious but didn't blame everyone and allowed us to continue when most of us thought we would be thrown out on our ears.

One of the memories I carried away from that year's filming with the Princess was that not once did she ever ask any of us, either during or after filming a particular sequence, 'How was I?' Having at that time been a professional interviewer for more than twenty years, I had invariably been asked by my subjects if everything had gone all right. She was supremely uninterested in our opinion of her and also in her own image and the way it was being portrayed. Even when the programme was finished—it set a precedent by being the first hour-long documentary to be screened on Independent Television without being interrupted by commercials—she never asked for confirmation of her, or its, success. It was a personal revelation of a very Royal trait.

The problems arise when television reporters, with their inevitable deadlines, need to know in advance if they are going to get the all-important interview. The Save the Children Fund would ideally like to schedule the interviews into the official programme so that they can tell the Press that they will definitely get them. This the Princess refuses to let them do. While it is true that she has given interviews at the conclusion of every overseas tour so far, they all happen at the eleventh hour, which is unsatisfactory for everyone involved except her. The Princess believes she is right and that it is unnecessary for those following her to have advance information. 'It is simply not true that I do not give television interviews during these tours. I believe it's fair to say that I have spoken to the Press on every single occasion. What I object to is having microphones stuck in my face as soon as I arrive in a country, before I have had time to look around and form any opinions. I know that journalists have a job to do and they all want to be first, but my rule is that I try to give them all the same chance—at the end of the tour, when at least I have something that is hopefully useful to say.'

What everyone around her accepts, reporters and entourage alike, is that when she does allow the media access, she handles them superbly. So well, indeed, that by the time they have finished their interviews she usually has them eating out of her hand—until the next time she holds them up until the last minute.

She is also human enough to admit that 'It is nice when one reads something pleasant.' Where she and the media are totally at odds is in deciding what is private and what is legitimate public interest. The Princess genuinely believes that her riding (except in charity events) is a private pastime and should be respected as such. She also feels passionately that there is no reason why her children should be of interest to anyone outside the family and that they should therefore be excluded from the Royal limelight.

The difficulty arises when editors instruct their reporters and photographers to get stories that will appeal to their readers, and by that they mean

211

human interest. Pictures of Peter Phillips dressed as a member of his school's firefighting team, showing his grandparents, the Queen and the Duke of Edinburgh, around Gordonstoun, were seen in newspapers throughout the country. They were perfectly harmless, and rather endearing. But they were not the sort of pictures that would have pleased the Princess Royal. Nor does she care for shots of her daughter Zara being taken at horse shows. These are private occasions, she feels, and should be respected as such. She and the Press will never agree on what constitutes intrusive journalism and it is unlikely that the feelings of either side will change.

For practically the entire time she was married to Mark Phillips, the Princess was the object of intense Press scrutiny because of constant rumours of a possible break-up. It began shortly after the wedding, and continued, practically non-stop, until the day they were divorced. The running battle between Anne and the Press became so fierce at times that even innocuous questions came to be treated by her as subtle attempts to get her to say something contentious. So much so, that when she visited the United States in 1982 and was asked what she thought about the birth of Prince William, she gave a short, sharp reply that appeared on the surface to be very sour. The truth was that she had not been told officially of the birth and did not want to be caught out making an off-the-cuff remark that might rebound. They wanted an instant quote which she was not prepared to provide. Once she had learnt the facts from Buckingham Palace she expressed her pleasure at the event in the warmest terms, but it was too late and reporters in the USA named her 'the person we would least like to interview'.

Less than six months later, at the end of a gruelling six-country tour of Africa, many of the same newsmen were so impressed by her behaviour under the most appalling conditions that they changed their opinion of her completely. Some of them even went so far as to 'adopt' children in the undeveloped areas they visited as part of the Save the Children sponsorship scheme. The change of attitude was so dramatic that even the Princess was impressed, remarking at the end of the tour, 'I did notice my miraculous transformation.'

One of the main problems in the Princess Royal's relationship with the media is her total honesty. Unlike other public figures who know that in order to enhance their images they have to do and say things they do not necessarily believe in or approve of, she says precisely what she thinks at all times. And because she has never managed, or perhaps even tried, to throw off her natural suspicion of journalists, she has also never achieved the artfulness that, say, a politician develops to maintain the appearance of even a superficial love affair with the media. Her refusal to pretend has become the trademark of her relations with the Press.

On the occasions when she has given interviews to reporters they are usually restricted to matters relating to a particular charity or function she is supporting at that time. The normal procedure is to submit a list of questions in advance so that she can do her homework and prepare intelligent answers. This is not so that she can avoid any tricky situations. She is far too experienced to be caught

213

out, and her stock reply to any query that might place her in a compromising position is to say, 'I don't think that's of any great interest.' This is the stonewall behind which she hides when she wants to avoid giving a straight answer, and all attempts to repeat the question are met in the same way.

However, once an interview has been arranged—either at Gatcombe Park or, more usually, in her sitting-room on the second floor of Buckingham Palace—the meeting takes place with only the two people concerned present. The Princess's Private Secretary introduces the journalist into her presence and then leaves them alone, and when the interview is taking place, she rarely refuses outright to answer questions which might not have been agreed beforehand. She knows that any journalist worth his salt will try to get her to say something indiscreet and frequently she will turn the tables on the interviewer and raise other topics herself. Another of her favourite ploys is to seek the opinions of the journalist. Sometimes this puts the interviewer at ease, making him or her feel flattered, at other times it might throw them off course, which is the intention.

Two things are guaranteed to irritate the Princess Royal with regard to dealing with the media: lack of communication and being ill-prepared for unseen eventualities. She likes to be fully briefed about all the people she is going to meet and the places she is visiting, and she hates to have anything sprung on her without notice. Hosts are always warned not to ask her to 'say a few words' without first obtaining her agreement.

The Princess Royal does not make much use of the Buckingham Palace Press Office, though one of the Queen's Assistant Press Secretaries has the nominal responsibility for handling her media affairs. Most Press arrangements, however, are looked after by the Princess's own Private Secretary, Lieutenant Colonel Peter Gibbs. He does keep the Press Office informed of what they are doing and where they are going, but even on an extensive overseas tour, where there might be large interest from the Press, the Princess is rarely accompanied by anyone from the Press Office, which is the normal channel of communication between the media and Buckingham Palace. Thus where the Princess Royal is involved reporters frequently side-step the official route and go straight to her office. This works most of the time, and Peter Gibbs keeps his colleagues in the Press Office informed as a courtesy.

If television is involved, then the Press Office does make the arrangements as both the BBC and ITV have officials whose job it is to liaise with the Palace and through whom every request for interviews or filming is channelled. It can be a long and complicated business, and often the easiest part is when they actually get face to face with the Princess herself. The reaction of reporters and photographers once they have met the Princess Royal can be interesting. Most come away talking about her intelligence and sense of humour and her frankness during their talk.

Photographers nearly always say she is better-looking in the flesh than on film. Unlike Diana, Princess of Wales, the most photographed woman in the world, who seems incapable of being photographed badly, Anne is rarely flattered by her pictures. So it comes as something of a surprise to see a woman who can be quite beautiful in person when one expected someone far less attractive.

The Princess Royal has never had any trouble with the regional Press in Britain. They usually only see her when she is in their area on official duties and on those occasions she is on show and has no objection to their attentions. Nor do they suffer from the sort of pressure on them that their colleagues on the national papers have to cope with. They rarely have competitors breathing down their necks or editors who demand sensational stories and pictures every day. They are often grateful for any access to Royalty and accept whatever they are given. This does not mean they are less professional than their counterparts in London, it's just that in the provinces, readers look for more detail in Royal stories, and as space is not at so much of a premium, the reporter is able to devote more column inches to his Royal subject.

Another reason why the provincial Press have always appeared to give the Princess favourable coverage is that they see her only infrequently, whereas the Royal rat-pack in London used to be famous faces and, as a result, they always look for the newsworthy items, not just the fact that she is there.

These days the relationship between the Princess Royal and the Press appears to have settled down to a wary accommodation. Her very indifference to what they write about her has resulted in their respect, albeit grudging. Each side knows the rules and by and large obeys them. She will never enjoy the devotion that Diana, Princess of Wales takes for granted, and the Press know that there is little chance of her giving any of them that elusive and exclusive scoop they all long for. If the current trends continue, there will be an increasing demand for more Royal stories, and while that demand exists newspapers and their editors will see no reason to change their approach.

There are those who would claim we have already reached saturation point, with nothing further to be said about the Royal Family. The people who make these claims are, unfortunately for them, those who would most like to see a decline in the present feverish coverage, and, again unfortunately for them, this is simply not going to happen. There will always be one more story to be written, another tiny detail of Royal minutiae to be revealed to satisfy the voracious appetite of reporters and readers alike. And with the prospect of a proliferation of satellite and cable television stations, the competition will grow increasingly fierce in the ratings battles and circulation wars of the tabloid media. So for the foreseeable future we are still going to have specialist Royal watchers, all anxious for that elusive scoop that might make their fortunes. Photographers are still going to spend thousands of pounds on sophisticated equipment to enable them to get that single shot that will put them into the super-tax bracket.

The Princess Royal doesn't often provide the Press with headlines, and even more rarely are they about her personal life. James Whitaker had the best story so far published about her when he broke to the world the news of her impending separation from Mark Phillips. Perhaps he is the right person to sum up the feelings of the Press for the Royal Family. 'Editors and reporters, we're all alike in this. If the Royals are nice to us we all roll over on our backs and want our tummies rubbed.'

The relationship between Palace and Press may be going through a period of comparative peace at the present time, but somehow I feel that James and his colleagues will have a long wait before the Princess Royal performs that particular service for any of them.

CHAPTER FOURTEEN

CELEBRITY PALS

Like many other members of the Royal Family, the Princess Royal is not averse to mixing with celebrities from many fields. As a young woman, before she became an internationally famous horsewoman in her own right, she was noticeably star-struck with the leading riders of the day, and now, in her mid-forties, she still enjoys the company of top movie stars and sporting giants.

She will also, unashamedly, use her own considerable influence to make sure these big names turn up for one of her own charitable events or for one organized by one of her select band of really close friends. Such is the case at the Celebrity Challenge Day held every year at Gleneagles in Scotland and organized by the former World Champion racing driver Jackie Stewart. As seen in Chapter 9, Stewart and his wife Helen have been friends with the Princess for more than twenty years, since he and she first met when they were voted sports personalities of the year in 1971. Her Royal Highness is a loyal friend and when Jackie Stewart, who has top-level connections of his own among the world's leading sports figures, asked her to appear at the first of his Celebrity Challenges, she immediately agreed. He knew this would give him and his event a seal of approval that no money could buy, and the Princess, who knows to a penny the value of her name, readily allowed it to be used in a good cause.

Since then other world-famous figures have fallen over themselves to accept Jackie Stewart's invitations, and in 1994 the Princess was present again, even though it meant she had to decline an invitation to the society wedding of the year, that of Prince Pavlov, son of King Constantine of The Hellenes, and American heiress Marie-Chantal Miller. Princess Anne had been at every one of Jackie Stewart's Celebrity Challenge Days since they started some twenty-one years earlier and she was not about to miss this one.

Jackie was delighted, of course, saying, 'The Princess Royal has been so loyal to us. She hasn't missed one.'

The presence of Her Royal Highness, plus stars of the calibre of Sean Connery, Tom Conti and Cheryl Ladd, and sporting figures such as racing driver Nigel Mansell, Scotland's rugby captain, Gavin Hastings, together with opera star Dame Kiri te Kanawa, ensured that the day was bound to be a brilliant success.

Mark Phillips competed in the Land-Rover team while Tim Laurence, rapidly adapting to the role of Royal consort, picked up one of the main prizes. As he was handed his award by his wife he also received a kiss, while her son Peter and ex-husband Mark Phillips had to be content with a friendly

219

handshake each.

The day's events included competitions in golf and clay pigeon shooting, and such was the skill of Jackie Stewart in assembling this fantastic mix of royals, aristocrats, sportsmen and movie stars— said to be one of the biggest collections of egos Scotland had ever seen—that just about everyone present, from the Duke of York to Lady Northampton, went home with a prize. It was all very jolly and sophisticated, with the world's leading glossy magazine *Hello!* there to make sure all the celebrities received their due publicity, and at the end of the day some £450,000 had been raised for charity.

The Princess Royal mingled with the other guests at a gala reception, and at the required photocall to mark the occasion she found herself seated, in the front row of course, between Jackie Stewart and Sean Connery, with her husband a couple of seats away next to Prince Andrew. Mark Phillips, on the other hand, was relegated to the extreme end of the third row. However, he was in quite good company alongside actor Tom Conti, singer Chris de Burgh and diva Kiri te Kanawa. Another old friend of the Princess, the actor Anthony Andrews, was also in the third row, but at the other end.

CHAPTER FIFTEEN

A COMPETITIVE HORSEWOMAN

The Royal Family are all either patrons or active participants in a variety of sporting pastimes, with each member choosing a different activity. The Queen loves racing—it's the overriding passion of her off-duty moments—while Prince Philip has concentrated on carriage-driving since his polo-playing days ended due to arthritis in his wrists. The Duke of York is a golf fanatic, while Prince Edward has revived interest in the Royal pastime of real tennis, playing on the courts once used by King Henry VIII at Hampton Court Palace. Close friends have said that the single most important thing in the life of the Prince of Wales is polo, and it is certainly true that for many years his staff organized his yearly programme around his polo engagements, at least until he was forced to retire from top-class competition following a serious injury.

Diana, Princess of Wales loves tennis, playing most weeks, summer and winter, and when she is not playing herself she likes to mix with the leading players of the day. In the past, every Wimbledon saw her in the Royal Box almost every day of the two-week tournament. The Duchess of York is a superb skier and swimmer and Queen Elizabeth the Queen Mother, now well into her tenth decade, remains a dedicated and skilful freshwater angler.

But if there is a single member of the Royal Family who is identified with one particular sport it is the Princess Royal. Since she entered the international sporting arena in 1971 she has become totally identified with Three-Day Eventing, one of the toughest of all equestrian sports.

Like all her family, she was introduced to riding at an early age, and horses have been her main sporting interest ever since. But that does not mean she concentrates on equestrianism to the exclusion of all other sports. She has tried most of them; some have remained in favour while others, such as fishing, which she tried in Scotland as a young girl, have failed to capture her imagination. She says the reason she does not care for fishing is not that she objects to standing up to her thighs in icy water for hours on end, as her grandmother Queen Elizabeth will do, it's just that she is not the most patient of women and a sport needs to be fast-moving to keep her attention.

Skiing was also a childhood sport, but unlike the Waleses and Yorks, she abandoned it after a brief adolescent flirtation until much later in life. In fact, she said she had only been skiing three times before she was eighteen and then did not go again until she was thirty-five, an age many people consider far too old to become proficient. But other people's opinions have rarely swayed the Princess Royal, and when her first husband, who was already a strong skier having competed in Alpine sports when he was in the Army, decided he wanted to continue, she joined in without hesitation. Her natural fitness helped a great deal so she did not have to undergo any special training first. Skiing is a sport that needs constant practice if one is to become, and remain, competent, and this the Princess is unable to do because of her other commitments, but her children also enjoy the sport and every winter they all, second husband Tim included, spend a holiday on the slopes at the French resort of Morzine or one of the other nearby centres. They have also been known to venture further afield, on to the less fashionable slopes in Norway.

Another winter sport which did not last for the Princess was ice skating. When she was still a schoolgirl being taught privately at Buckingham Palace, she and the girls who took their lessons with her would be given the exclusive use of Richmond Ice Rink whenever they paid a visit. But the attraction didn't last and the only occasion when the Princess Royal showed any enthusiasm for ice skating was in 1984 when as President of the British Olympic Association she cheered Jayne Torvill and Christopher Dean as they won a Gold Medal for Britain in Sarajevo, at the Winter Olympic Games.

The Princess is also a keen and expert sailor. She is an active President of the Royal Yachting Association and regularly visits Cowes during regatta week, along with her father and younger brother, Prince Edward. It was Prince Philip who taught her to sail, and in 1992 she bought a five-berth, sea-going cruising yacht which she and Tim use in the summer months. Peter and Zara have inherited their mother's love of the sea and they have both completed Royal Yachting Association sailing courses.

One of the many advantages of being born Royal is that whatever you want to try you can, and where sport is concerned, the world's leading professionals are available for advice and encouragement. Such was the case when Princess Anne was going through her tennis phase. There was a period in her teens when she played little else, though she says this was because 'It was considered good for me', rather than from any particular love of the game. She was introduced to tennis by none other than the late Dan Maskell, doyen of Wimbledon commentators, and a man who had seen most of the leading players of the century. He coached her for a time and actually said he thought she could have reached Wimbledon standard if she had kept it up and been prepared to devote her life to it. After all, her grandfather, King George VI, was passionately fond of the game and even played in a doubles match at the world's number one tournament, so there was a family tradition of sorts.

In his autobiography, *From Where I Sit*, Maskell explained in some detail how he came to be involved with Princess Anne's introduction to tennis.

I was taken up to the nursery where I met Miss Peebles [the governess]. Anne and two other girls about her own age [Caroline Hamilton and Sukie Babington-Smith] were just finishing their lesson ... Miss Peebles sent them off to change and I was taken down to a bedroom on the garden side of the palace near the swimming pool. When I had changed ... I waited on the patio outside ... At that first lesson it was obvious that Anne was blessed with natural ball sense. Her companions were less gifted but I took care to see there was no favouritism. I paid about half a dozen visits to the palace on

Monday mornings in the spring and summer that year ... Anne quickly outstripped the other two and it was clear she would have benefited from individual lessons. The following year she did have lessons by herself. Anne was a natural athlete and a good, strong mover around the court ... We were now rallying and enjoying keeping each other on the move ... The service proved a little more difficult, as it does with so many girls.

Maskell showed his pupil how to learn to throw the ball high into the air and then launch the racket head at it. He said that after another two or three lessons she was beginning to get the hang of it. He then summed up his feelings about her playing skills.

In the course of those few sessions it had become clear that Anne had the ability, if she so wished, and if it had been appropriate to spend the necessary time at the game, to compete on the international circuit. When we started to play a few actual games in our sessions, I was aware of a keen competitive spirit which was later revealed in her riding activities.

Maskell also saw that competitive element in her character when they used to swim together in the palace pool after the tennis lessons. On one occasion they were joined by Prince Charles (who was also having tennis lessons) and they challenged Maskell to a race.

They seemed to me to revel in the water,

swimming around like fishes . . . they insisted we should have a race the length of the pool and I asked how much start they would give me. Prince Charles said, 'All right, you go first, then Anne will go and then I'll chase you both . . .' they had both passed me before I was halfway down the pool.

Years later, when I spoke to the Princess about her tennis skills, she was self-deprecatingly sceptical, saying, 'I think Dan Maskell was being diplomatically kind and anyway, I know I am temperamentally unsuited to the game. I do not like the single confrontation aspect, and the cauldron-like atmosphere of Wimbledon and the other major venues does not appeal to me at all.' She later told commentator Gerald Williams, when he asked her if she was likely to be seen that year in the Royal Box at Wimbledon, 'Not this year or any other.'

Everyone in the Royal Family swims. They have all been taught properly and the Princess learned the basics when she was very young, in the pool at Buckingham Palace, though she did not have the unpleasant experience of her older brother Charles who was forced by his father to jump into the water and told to 'get on with it'. Princess Anne was given professional instruction in how to breathe correctly, and even though she claims to dislike swimming as a form of exercise 'unless desperate', her style is adequate, conventional and economical, which means she can keep going for long periods if necessary. There is no swimming pool at Gatcombe Park; the nearest thing they have is a pool that was installed in the stable block for the horses which is used to help cure injuries. When it was being built, the Press had a field day, claiming that Anne and Mark had spent thousands of pounds on a 'swimming pool for their horses'. All totally untrue but a good story none the less.

Shooting is another traditional Royal sport but the ladies do not shoot; they act as 'pickers up' for the men. This is also a skill that needs to be learnt and the Queen is said to be an expert. The Princess Royal also knows how to work her two gun dogs brilliantly and her shooting days at Gatcombe are full of good sport. With Tim Laurence's help, she organizes the entire day, allocates the shooting positions for the guns, and everybody seems to go home fully satisfied when she's in charge. Her close friend Jackie Stewart is a marksman of near-Olympic standard and he enjoys few things more than a day's shooting in the company of his favourite Royal. The Princess also arranged for his two sons to be introduced to the sport at an early age.

Horses have been the mainstay of the Princess's sporting interests throughout her life, however, and she has become one of the world's outstanding riders in what is without doubt one of the most demanding of all equestrian disciplines. The decision to pursue eventing seriously, as opposed to treating it merely as a part-time rich girl's hobby, was taken quite deliberately by the Princess. She was desperate to see if there was something she could do really well, and wanted to test herself on equal terms against other competitors who would not give her any quarter just because of her birth.

However, even if the other riders were unconcerned about her Royal pedigree, some of the hosts at major events were all too aware of who was taking part on their land, and made sure she did not have to suffer any discomforts. When she competed at Badminton, Chatsworth or Burghley, Princess Anne never had to bother about finding digs in the area or stay in one of the mobile homes that parked in the caravan villages near the course, like other competitors. She was invariably lodged in the 'big house' in very comfortable rooms, which was convenient for her and her security officers, but also meant that she was distanced from the other riders and did not experience the camaraderie that develops among competitors who rough it together.

Until the Princess entered the sport, Three-Day Eventing was a comparatively little-known activity, confined in the main to the sons and daughters of landowners, well-to-do farmers and members of the more fashionable cavalry regiments. The general public knew nothing about the sport, and television was a long way from discovering it as one of the great spectacles of the seventies and eighties. Even the Badminton Horse Trials, then as now the world's leading Three-Day Event, could attract only a few thousand dedicated supporters, and the sport's reputation as being only for a wealthy elite was not only well deserved but jealously guarded by those who ran it.

Nobody, inside the sport or outside, could have guessed at the impact one young woman would have. Within three short years advertisers would fight among themselves to pour hundreds of thousands of pounds into eventing, the BBC would invest millions in television coverage, and Three-Day Events would receive prime-time exposure, not only in Britain but throughout the world. Riders such as Richard Meade, Lucinda Prior-Palmer (later Green) and Mark Phillips would become household names, and as the advertising opportunities became apparent, big-name agents like Mark McCormack came on to the scene to exploit the commercial possibilities. The sport would retain its elitist reputation, and up-market firms such as Simpson and Asprey cashed in on the affluent patronage by investing thousands of pounds in building temporary stores in the trade villages which sprang up at each international event. Where once the organizers thought themselves fortunate if they managed to get a few hundred pounds' worth of sponsorship, suddenly multinational companies were falling over themselves to throw money at them. Land-Rover became one of the biggest and most successful of Three-Day Event sponsors, with several of the major drinks companies not far behind.

Television elevated the sport to a prime-time spectacular, and this in turn attracted hundreds of thousands more supporters who attended events in person. And the one person they all wanted to see was Princess Anne—especially if she fell off at the water jump! It became a matter of pride among newspaper photographers to see who could get the best picture of her in the most undignified position, though it would only be fair to point out that she was dumped in the lake at Badminton just once during her career and on no more than four occasions at other courses. Nevertheless, that first picture of her getting soaked at Badminton was recorded by 150 photographers and appeared in newspapers and magazines throughout the world.

229

If she had been just another rider it would have been completely ignored, but she wasn't, and she was realistic enough to know that it was just part of the price she had to pay for being Royal. As she told me, 'Horses are no respecters of rank and when I'm approaching a water jump with two thousand people watching and a couple of hundred photographers waiting for me to be thrown in, the horse is the only one who doesn't know I'm Royal.'

This was all very much in the future in 1968, which was when the Princess entered the sport for the first time, having competed at many Pony Club events as a youngster. At the time a number of prominent people in the equestrian world thought that if she were to enter seriously it would be as a show-jumper not an eventer. Show-jumping was the more glamorous side of the sport and even then stars like David Broome and Harvey Smith had become famous in Britain and abroad. The Princess knew both these horsemen, and many others, and regularly went to Wembley and Olympia for the International Horse Shows. She loved being around the horsey set; they were her kind of people. She was impressed by their seeming nonchalance and even their cavalier attitude to what passes for good manners among outsiders. She went so far as attempting to emulate their language, swearing like a trooper, though in her case it didn't quite come off. It seemed as if she had learnt to use four-letter words rather later in life than most people and when she swore it sounded as if she was putting the words in deliberately for effect. Some of the older show-jumpers found it an endearing trait and were quietly amused. As Mark Twain put it when describing his wife's attempts at profanity, 'She knows all the right words, but she has yet to learn the tunes.' There is of course nothing new about members of the Royal Family using coarse language, as visitors to Clarence House and Kensington Palace have often found out.

The reason why the Princess did not choose show-jumping to make her sporting mark was because, even at eighteen, she had started to take on a large number of public engagements and her official programme simply would not allow her enough time for training and competing at top level. Eventing was a natural progression from hunting which she had done since she was a child, so it followed that she should take it up when she decided she wanted to do something seriously in sport.

It has also been suggested that as she had always been something of a loner she was better suited to a sport where it was a matter of just her and the horse against the course, rather than working as a member of a team. This theory does not really hold water as the same thing could have applied if she had become a show-jumper or a tennis player. And indeed, when she did eventually reach the top, competing at European and Olympic level, it was as a member of the British team and not as an individual.

She gave a perfect example of her team spirit in 1976 when she was taking part in the Montreal Olympic Games. She fell badly on the cross-country course and suffered massive concussion, only to remount and complete the course without knowing where she was. As she put it, 'The lights were on but there was no one at home.' Afterwards

231

she said, 'I was riding as a member of the team so there was no question of quitting.'

Once Alison Oliver had agreed to become her trainer, after a careful looking-over, Anne would drive herself from Buckingham Palace at seven o'clock in the morning to Alison's stables in Buckinghamshire for a three-hour session. She would then return to the Palace to prepare for the day's engagements and, if there were no evening commitments, drive back to the stables for another couple of hours at the end of the day. It was an arduous and tiring time but one which the Princess readily accepted, as she was determined to get to the top, even if Mrs Oliver did not at first think she was ready. 'I knew there was something there right from the start, but I didn't think, at the beginning, that she would become a champion as quickly as she did.'

From starting to event seriously to taking part in her first Badminton took just three years. By any standards it was a remarkable achievement. For a young woman who was also performing public duties at home and abroad, it was nothing short of miraculous. She began quietly enough in 1968 and then, in April the following year, riding her Irish horse, Royal Ocean, in section D of the Novices Trials at the Windsor Horse Trials, she moved into the big time. She won the event, beating twenty-six other competitors including a certain young Army Lieutenant named Mark Phillips—the only time she would ever do so.

Then began a hectic year of travelling the length and breadth of the country gaining valuable experience and building a solid reputation. She had started to be taken seriously by riders and officials alike, so when it was announced the following year that she had qualified to ride at Badminton, on her by now number one horse, Doublet, there was no criticism or surprise.

Forty-seven of the world's top riders assembled at the Duke of Beaufort's Gloucestershire estate in April 1971 and not one would have given their Royal colleague the slightest chance of being placed or even finishing the tough cross-country course with its thirty-one obstacles. However, at the end of the first day's dressage test, the Princess was in first place, and she finished the second day—over the cross-country course—fourth, well placed for the final day's show-jumping.

Although she had virtually no chance of winning—the three riders in front of her would have had to knock down three fences each and she would have needed to go clear—the Royal Family had turned out in force, with the Queen, the Duke of Edinburgh, the Queen Mother, Princess Margaret and Anne's three brothers, Charles, Andrew and Edward, all there to support her. They had plenty to cheer as Anne finished in a brilliant fifth place, the winner that year being Mark Phillips on Great Ovation. For the Princess and Doublet it was the start of their outstandingly successful partnership. Badminton had only been Princess Anne's second Three-Day Event—the previous ones had been One-Day—and Doublet's first. It all augured well.

A month later she heard that she had been chosen to compete in the European Championships at Burghley, but as an individual, not as a member of the British team. It was a well-deserved accolade but one which nearly backfired,

233

as shortly before the event Anne was suddenly taken ill and rushed to King Edward VII's Hospital for Officers (known as Sister Agnes's) in London. There she was operated on for the removal of an ovarian cyst, or as she put it, 'I had various revolting bits of me removed.'

Alison Oliver thought that meant the end of her Royal pupil's chances that year, but she had reckoned without Anne's courage and determination. Within weeks she was up and about, exercising her stomach muscles and walking up and down the hills around Balmoral to strengthen her legs and back. It wasn't all work, however. A twenty-first birthday party held on board the Royal Yacht *Britannia* provided some light relief and helped to ease the tension as Burghley approached. Even she admitted that 'For three nights I didn't sleep much before Burghley.'

The 1971 European Championships could not have gone better. Princess Anne went into an immediate lead in the dressage section, maintained it over the cross-country course and entered the final day's show-jumping in an unassailable position. The Queen and Prince Philip were there to see their daughter's triumph as she entered the arena. She could have afforded to knock down one fence and still win, but she did not need that cushion. A brilliant clear round had the capacity crowd on its feet cheering wildly as a delighted Princess Anne swept to the most popular victory the sport had ever seen. Her Majesty smiled broadly as she presented the Raleigh Trophy and a cheque for £250 to the winner, while Prince Philip, as President of the International Equestrian Federation, presented the medal. All in all it was a

234

great family occasion.

When I interviewed Princess Anne for BBC Television shortly after the ceremony, her delight was obvious, but even in that moment of high euphoria, her natural caution took over. When I asked about her ambitions for the following year's Olympic Games she refused to be drawn, saying it was all a long way off and it was too soon to make any definite predictions.

So at the age of twenty-one, Princess Anne had virtually become World Champion. It had been a meteoric rise to the top and no one would have blamed her if she had decided to retire right then. After all, she had done all that she had set out to do and there was nothing else to prove, either to herself or to others.

Some years later, in a conversation at Buckingham Palace, the Princess reflected that perhaps it had all happened too soon. 'Possibly it happened too early in my career. After Burghley there was the danger that I would fall away, because I had reached the top after just three years in the sport ... I did not really appreciate what we had achieved.'

Her ex-husband Mark Phillips, who knows a thing or two about competing at the highest level, thought that was absolute rubbish. 'Sport is all about winning and you have to take your chances when they come.' And, of course, one of the Princess Royal's Ladies-in-Waiting, Jane Holderness-Roddam, was even younger when she hit the top, being only eighteen when she rode in the 1968 Olympic Games.

Anne's success was warmly applauded by the media in 1971, when she was voted Sportswoman of the Year. World Champion Formula One racing driver Jackie Stewart shared the podium as he became Sportsman of the Year, and at the ceremony a friendship was forged that has lasted to this day.

The next hurdle on the horizon was the 1972 Olympics, but Doublet collapsed with tendon trouble which put paid to Anne's international ambitions in that direction until 1976 at least. She was fortunate in having another horse almost as good as Doublet coming along, and in 1973 Goodwill, which had been bought for the Princess by the Queen, helped Anne defend her European title in Kiev. Once again she had been selected to ride as an individual, not in the official British team, but this time her participation did not last long. At the notorious second fence on the cross-country course—made up of telegraph poles nailed together over a ditch—Anne got it completely wrong. There was an horrendous crash which she later described to me as 'like hitting tarmac... I had never hit the ground as hard or as fast ... when I got up I couldn't feel a thing, but I couldn't walk. I could stand on one leg but that was about all. Goodwill looked completely stunned.' There was no point in continuing; she wasn't riding as a team member so she retired and then discovered that her right shoulder was dislocated so badly that she has suffered a slight unevenness in that shoulder ever since. It is not a noticeable deformity but enough for her dressmaker to need to make tiny adjustments to her clothes to disguise it.

Horses were now playing a major part in the Princess's life, so much so that many people who met her in the course of her official duties thought that all they had to do to please her was to show her some horses. They were wrong. And when her Private Secretary carried out his regular recce visits prior to her engagements, he gently but firmly informed would-be hosts that the Princess was only really interested in her own horses and their performances, so they would be better advised not to try to include general equestrian matters in her programme.

With two excellent horses, Doublet and Goodwill, in her stable, the Princess found plenty to exercise her talents after her successes at Burghley and elsewhere. In between, in 1973, she married her foremost competitor, Mark Phillips, and they moved to married quarters at the Royal Military Academy at Sandhurst, which is where she learned to drive a lorry. She took her HGV (Heavy Goods Vehicle) licence and it was just a week later, following a horse trials in Gloucestershire, that she was forced to drive a horsebox on a public road for the first time. Mark had injured his back in the competition and could not drive, so Princess Anne took the wheel, and enjoyed the experience so much that afterwards she was frequently seen driving up and down the motorways of Great Britain. This gave rise to the belief that she had said that if she hadn't been a Princess she would have liked to be a long-distance lorry driver. It's a nice story but the truth is that she simply said that if she were not who she is she would be able to earn a living as a lorry driver. Not quite the same thing.

The year 1974 proved to be one of the most difficult in the Princess's life, both on and off the sports field. In March, she and Mark were the subject of an attempted kidnap (see Chapter 4); in

April, Doublet took part in his final competition at Badminton, and a few weeks later came what Princess Anne described as 'quite the most ghastly experience of my entire life'. While she was riding him quietly at Windsor one morning, Doublet broke a leg. There was nothing to be done except to put him out of his misery. Nothing had prepared the Princess for the loss and she was distraught, even though she later said that 'He was rather a difficult horse to get to know. He wasn't a particularly friendly horse. He was rather aloof and one rather admired him for it. But he wasn't a horse you could go and chat to.' Lady Susan Hussey, who saw the Princess a few hours after Doublet had been put down, said, 'She was inconsolable and completely shattered.'

1975 saw Anne selected as part of the first all-female team to compete in the European Championships. They were held at Lumuhlen in what was then West Germany, and the four girls, Lucinda Prior-Palmer, Janet Hodgson, Sue Hatherly and Princess Anne, more than justified their selection. Lucinda won the individual Gold Medal, and Princess Anne the Silver, with the team taking the group Silver Medal. It was the most successful British team to take part in these championships and a particularly satisfying performance for the Princess. She later said that winning the Silver at Lumuhlen was better in some ways than taking the Gold at Burghley.

The following year Anne was selected for the British team for the Montreal Olympic Games, with Mark relegated to reserve. They travelled with the rest of the team, in economy class, and stayed in the Olympic Village in exactly the same type of accommodation as the other athletes. Princess Anne had made it clear that she would vigorously resist any attempts by officialdom to segregate her from her team-mates or to treat her as anything other than an ordinary member of the squad.

The Games were not successful either for the team or for the Princess as an individual. She took a bad fall on the cross-country course and was badly concussed, but refused to quit as, unlike in Kiev, she was competing here as part of the team; the idea of giving up simply did not arise. She ended the competition in twenty-fourth place and since that day has never again reached international status.

She had had a magnificent career, winning the European Championships at her first attempt, being the only rider to win medals on different horses (Doublet and Goodwill), being part of the official British team in Europe and at the Olympic Games, and completing Badminton no fewer than five times, for which she was awarded a plaque. She continued to compete in the United Kingdom and occasionally abroad, but as the sport became increasingly professional she has been unable to devote the time and energy to training and also she has never found another Doublet or Goodwill. She was a brilliant horsewoman, tough, uncompromising and determined, with a single-mindedness that took her to the top in a remarkably short period.

Princess Anne's association with horses was not over, however, and as she looked for new challenges, she found them in an area she had not previously considered—racing. Nine years after the '76 Olympics, she had her first outing on the Flat.

It was a mile-and-a-half race over the Derby course at Epsom and she had been invited to ride as the proceeds were going to one of her favourite charities, Riding for the Disabled. She accepted immediately, believing it was to be her first and last race, and began preparing at David Nicholson's yard at Condicote. This is some forty minutes' drive from Gatcombe, and in order to be in time for 'early stables' at seven o'clock, the Princess had to get up at 5.30 a.m. and leave just after six.

The horse chosen for her was Against the Grain and they came a creditable fourth. More importantly, the race raised over £30,000 for RDA. The Princess had been bitten by the bug and she couldn't wait to get back into the saddle as a lady jockey. But it wasn't until 5 August 1986 that she rode her first winner. The race was at Redcar and Anne was on Gulfland. As she swept past the winning post it looked as if she was going to keep going around the course again. This was because she was obeying Nicholson's number one rule, 'Never look around and make sure you are well past the winning post before you relax.' 'Duke' Nicholson is not a man who is easily intimidated and his Royal rider did not frighten him in the least. He was as tough with her as he was with any of his jockeys, but he recognized her particular difficulties. 'It's bad enough for anyone who takes this business seriously, but for her it's twice as bad.'

Since that first win, she has notched up a further five firsts, with ten second places and numerous lesser positions. Not content with being accepted on the Flat, the Princess then turned her attention to the tougher discipline of National Hunt Rules— her grandmother's favourite form of racing. Josh

Gifford, an old friend of David Nicholson, found her the right horse in Cnoc na Cuille, and she had her first ride over the jumps at Kempton on 20 February 1986, coming fourth. Six more races on the same horse gave her the experience and confidence she needed when she rode out at Worcester on 3 September 1987. In a small field the Princess took the lead in the final furlong, beating the odds-on favourite by half a length. She later said it was the most satisfying race of her entire career. She also told an anecdote which shows how she can stand up for herself. In the car park after the race she was accosted by an irate punter who had lost money by her winning. He was mumbling about the race being fixed. The Princess left her police bodyguard standing near her car and walked alone over to the man and told him that she was not the person to complain to if he really believed the race had been fixed and he had no business taking his anger out on her. Eventually they parted on reasonably good terms.

The win at Worcester proved to be the only success the Princess had under National Hunt Rules despite over forty rides. But she enjoyed herself and once again had proved that on horseback there were few things she could not attempt. Andrew Parker Bowles reckons that the reason she took up racing in the first place was because of the danger. 'She had always liked the physical aspect of racing, the danger and the challenge. She loves a challenge and she wanted to prove to herself that she could do it. She is a remarkable horsewoman, much better all round than the Prince of Wales and totally without fear. She was both a horsewoman and a jockey which is unusual in that one is normally one or the other. She never had the choice of the best horses, yet in spite of that she rode some very good races. When you think that she has had to fit her racing into her official programme it speaks volumes for her dedication and her fitness. Most riders are riding out three or four days a week, she was lucky to get the odd day in when she could.' Andrew also feels that as her competitive days draw to a close she still has a great deal to offer the sport. 'You have to remember that she has earned a tremendous amount of respect, not only as someone who can raise funds and organize committees, but also as a jockey who knows the problems of the riders. She has actually done it and nobody can take that away from her.'

When she reflected on what she regarded as her greatest contribution to racing, the Princess Royal exhibited a wry sense of humour by claiming that she had managed to get major improvements to the facilities for lady jockeys. When she started there were virtually no separate changing-rooms, showers or baths. The ladies all had to cope as best they could in somewhat primitive conditions. She said that by the time she had finished, she had at least got them more lavatories!

CHAPTER SIXTEEN

PRESIDENT ANNE?

There have been a number of surveys in the past few years, particularly since the break-up of the marriage of the Prince and Princess of Wales, which have all placed the Princess Royal as the person the majority of those polled would prefer to be the next Sovereign. It has become such an accepted opinion, even though it is never going to happen, that when yet another poll reveals the same results, no one takes much notice these days.

However, a survey conducted for the *Guardian* newspaper, not noted for its Royalist views, about the Monarchy and its future, included questions about which members of the Royal Family were considered to be 'doing a good job'. The Princess Royal received a massive vote of confidence with 67 per cent of those polled claiming she is worthwhile. The only person to achieve a higher rating was the Queen with 72 per cent. And when asked who has most damaged the Monarchy, the Princess Royal was not even mentioned. Nobody thought she had ever done a thing to harm the institution.

Another newspaper poll about who would be the people's most popular choice for President if Britain became a republic, caused great surprise in many quarters when the name that emerged as the overall favourite was that of the Princess Royal. Even Rabbi Julia Neuberger, who herself came sixth in the poll, was reported to have said later that she would have voted for the Princess.

The Princess Royal, that most regal of all Royal Princesses, the one person of her generation within the Royal Family who has never done anything to undermine the Monarchy and who, equally, has never for a moment doubted the validity of our present hereditary system, as Britain's first President? The poll confirmed what many people

243

have thought about the Princess for years. She is easily the most respected member of the Royal Family; her work for her many charities and the way in which she is able to conduct herself with world leaders on a one-to-one basis, without once putting a foot wrong, leads one to believe that perhaps it is not such a fantastic notion after all.

Although to many people the Princess Royal might appear to be the least likely candidate for the Presidency, this would not be on the basis of her inability to do the job. She never leaves this country for one of her overseas tours without being fully briefed, and neither her intelligence nor her courage to face danger and the unknown has ever been in doubt. When she meets Presidents and Prime Ministers in any part of the world, it is not merely a courtesy call where platitudes are the order of the day. She makes serious points and argues her case, or, more correctly, the case of the organization she is representing at the time, even if she knows that what she is saying is not exactly what the other party wants to hear.

For the last twenty-five years the Princess has been alone performer on the world's stage. Travelling hundreds of thousands of miles every year, she journeys to parts of the world other members of the Royal Family would never dream of visiting. The more remote and unwelcoming the terrain, the more attractive it becomes to her. If there is a little bit of danger attached, it does not put her off. She is not foolish enough deliberately to put herself at risk, but on those occasions where she has weighed up the perils of going where the Foreign Office has strongly advised her not to go, she usually ends up doing the opposite of what they

244

suggest. This does not endear her to officialdom; but then again, she has never been one to worry unduly about the opinions of others—apart from her parents'.

She acknowledges that on many of her overseas trips the locals rarely recognize her or even know who she is. It is not in the least bit important to her 'as long as the Fund [Save the Children] benefits'. And it is not in just the undeveloped Third World countries that this happens. On a fund-raising trip to the USA on behalf of the British Olympic Association, she encountered a bewildering array of civic dignitaries in Houston, one of whom told her, 'You look just like your sister, the Queen.' Her Royal Highness didn't turn a hair, she merely thanked him politely and moved on. On another occasion a Texas millionaire remarked that it was a great pity she wasn't allowed to marry her boyfriend, Peter Townsend—another example of her being confused with other members of her family, this time her aunt, Princess Margaret.

The Princess Royal has built a protective shell around herself in order not to show any form of emotion in public. This sometimes gives the impression that she does not care. When she sees tiny children dying of malnutrition and disease she rarely displays any feelings of pity or sorrow. But as she herself has said, 'It's not going to do anybody any good if I just stand there wringing my hands. It's the practical effort we put into solving the problems that's going to do some good and that's what I'm concerned with.'

But she does care, and the sights she has seen have made a lasting impression on her. The only time in recent years that members of her staff have seen her reduced to tears was following her first visit to Auschwitz concentration camp. After seeing the evidence of the Holocaust, in particular the thousands of tiny shoes torn from the feet of infants and the piles of baby clothes, the Princess was visibly moved, and later, back in the privacy of her hotel room, she gave way and the tears flowed. Her years of training had allowed her to stay dry-eyed throughout the tour and while the television cameras were on her, but afterwards the emotion showed.

The most recent occasion when her public face slipped slightly was when she accompanied the Queen to Dunblane after the massacre of sixteen children had horrified the world. Her Majesty asked her daughter to go with her, appropriately enough on Mother's Day, and together they paid tribute to the memory of the children and their teacher who had died when a man burst into their school gymnasium and murdered most of the class of five-year-olds. The Queen and the Princess Royal shared the grief of the bereaved townspeople, with Anne leaving a tiny bunch of snowdrops she had picked in her own garden at Gatcombe that morning. Her card read simply: 'From all my family, Anne.' Both she and her mother shed a tear as they were caught up in the wave of grief that swept over the town, and it was significant that it was the Princess who was invited personally by the Queen and no one else.

You will never hear Anne say she wants to be a 'Queen of Hearts' or demand an ambassadorial role from the Government, as her sister-in-law, Diana, Princess of Wales, has done so publicly on television. Few would doubt, however, that she, more than any other member of her family, is qualified to represent Britain abroad as an official or unofficial ambassador. In the years she has been carrying out her public duties she has become one of the most experienced women in the world in matters of health care and education, famine relief and world poverty. In addition she represents the Queen on many occasions, handling delicate missions with tact, dignity and good humour. In short, she has learned her trade; she has served her apprenticeship, and through sheer dedication and hard work over nearly three decades, she fully deserves the respect she now enjoys.

Her courage has never been in doubt, and she does not flinch from saying what she thinks. As Patron of the Butler Trust, she visits prisons throughout the country observing how the service is run. But she is under no illusions about the 'clients' in the institutions she goes to, saying on one occasion that most of the inmates of Britain's prisons are 'as innocent as Stalin'. It is refreshing to hear someone of her stature speak out without thoughts of political correctness to harness her words.

Like both her parents, but unlike her brother Charles and his ex-wife, the Princess Royal has always believed it is not necessary to be personally popular in order to be successful. What is important is to secure and retain the respect of the people, not their slavish devotion. The Queen has been the perfect example of this attitude since she came to the throne. Her Majesty does not inspire the sort of relationship with her people that, say, the Queen Mother does. Nor would she ever wish to. Her method is to remain slightly aloof, sympathetic but above all regal, and no Sovereign has been more successful than Elizabeth II has in the past forty-five years.

Princess Anne works on the same principle. She does her work as professionally as she is able, knowing that few people can justifiably criticize her in terms of her workload. It has been a long, hard climb to reach the position she now enjoys as the most admired member of her generation in the Royal Family.

Respected and appreciated as she undoubtedly is, however, it would be interesting, if there were to be a change in Britain's constitution from Monarchy to Republic, to see how many of those people who voted for the Princess Royal as a possible future President in a newspaper survey, would actually do so in real life. It's all very well to say you want a particular figure as your leader when there isn't the remotest chance of it happening. But how would her supporters prepare her campaign in the unlikely event that she would even allow her name to be proposed? Why bother to get rid of the present system of selecting a Head of State, if all we want to do is replace the incumbent with her own daughter, especially as that daughter has always supported her mother totally and has never criticized the manner in which she has reigned over the country by so much as a whisper.

The Anne for President group could claim that because she is who she is, she would be the one person in the country who could honestly say she was above party politics. Nobody has ever known how the Princess votes, or even if she does exercise her franchise. Most people assume that the entire

248

Royal Family, because of their upper-class lineage, are true blue, natural Conservatives, with ultra-right-wing leanings, to whom the idea of voting Labour would be anathema. If the personal standing of the Queen's various Prime Ministers is anything to go by, this could be far from the truth. While Winston Churchill held a very special place in Her Majesty's affections, that was not because of his political views but purely as the result of his own personality and charisma. Of the more recent PMs, James Callaghan (now Lord Callaghan of Cardiff) appears to have had by far the closest relationship with the Queen and has remained friends with her long after leaving office. No one has ever accused him of having leanings towards the Conservatives.

One of the Queen's greatest attributes is the fact that in over forty years on the throne she has been able to meet and talk with the leaders of all the Commonwealth countries, including Britain, despite their vastly different political affiliations which range from Marxist to near-Fascist. Similarly, the Princess Royal is apolitical and is arguably one of the handful of public personalities in Britain who could justifiably claim to have no party connections of any kind. So she might be exactly the right person for Head of State if we were to become a republic.

In 1990 the Princess Royal was nominated for the Nobel Peace Prize, and in a distinguished field was narrowly defeated by the then Soviet leader, Mikhail Gorbachev. The man who submitted her name was Lord Callaghan. Before compiling his letter to the Nobel Committee in Oslo, he did a tremendous amount of research on the Princess's background as a worker for an international relief agency and even asked the leaders of a number of Commonwealth countries for their comments on his proposal. Presidents Kenneth Kaunda of Zambia and Robert Mugabe of Zimbabwe were not only enthusiastic in their support but allowed their names to be attached to the nomination. Lord Callaghan also spoke to the Queen and Prince Philip about his intentions, without asking for their help. It was merely a courtesy on his part as he had no wish to involve them in what might have been seen as unseemly lobbying for their daughter. And the Princess was kept completely in the dark; she had no idea of the campaigning that was going on on her behalf.

In the final draft of the letter Lord Callaghan sent he confined himself to the main points of a career in public service.

The Princess Royal began her world-wide involvement in famine relief, child care and education in under-developed countries of the world when she accepted the Presidency of the Save the Children Fund on 1 January 1970, which means ... she is therefore the longest-serving President of any international charity in the world.

From the moment she became its President, the Princess has taken an active role in all its many activities, travelling throughout every country where the Fund is allowed to operate. In terms of finance alone she has been responsible for increasing the income of the Fund from £50,000 a year when she started, to more than £50 million a year today ... that is a proud record and one that is freely attributed to the leadership of Her Royal Highness.

She has become totally identified with Save the Children, both in Europe and throughout Africa and South East Asia, where her efforts have been applauded by Presidents, Prime Ministers, politicians of every persuasion and, more importantly, by the people her Fund has been able to help.

The Princess Royal has studied the problems of famine relief, child care and basic hygiene at first hand and she is now as knowledgeable about the problems as any of the professional field workers, whose primitive conditions she willingly shares when she visits them . . .

Her Royal Highness was the first member of the Royal Family to visit refugee camps in Lebanon, the first to enter what is claimed to be the poorest region in the world, and the first to offer practical help in Bangladesh.

Throughout her long and distinguished association with the Save the Children Fund she has worked tirelessly to promote a fuller understanding of the problems facing Third World countries, without any thought for her own personal safety or comfort . . . and never in the past twenty years has she once used her position for anything other than the benefit of the causes she espouses.

The fact that she has been so single-minded in her pursuit of better understanding between nations has meant that she has allowed no political expediency to stand in the way of progress as far as the welfare of the children is concerned. This has been her only goal and her achievements, which have not always received the publicity they deserved in her own country, are regarded as significant in the extreme in those countries which have benefited.

Nothing could better sum up the work of the Princess Royal for just one of her many charities than this letter from one of the world's leading statesmen. The fact that she did not receive the Nobel Prize was a considerable disappointment; not to her personally, though naturally, she would have been pleased to accept the honour, but the workers in her many organizations and the political leaders throughout the world who supported her nomination all felt that the time was right for some sort of international recognition for a woman who had never sought honours for herself. As far as she was concerned, though, it was business as usual. She had not been aware of the campaign being fought on her behalf and had she been informed beforehand, she would have made strenuous efforts to dissuade her would-be promoters, although privately she would have been extremely flattered by their attentions.

When the Princess changed from being Patron of Riding for the Disabled to becoming its President, the late Lavinia, Duchess of Norfolk, who had been President until then, and who suggested the change, said, 'Being Patron seems to imply that she is just a figurehead, a Royal name on our letterheads. Nothing could be further from the truth where Princess Anne [as she was then] is concerned. She involves herself in every aspect of our work, chairs committees and oversees all key appointments. So it is appropriate that she should become President with all the executive responsibilities that the title implies.'

The Princess Royal has become a past master in the art of compromise, which many people believe is completely at odds with her natural inclinations, thinking her to be totally inflexible. But as she herself told me, 'I've been a professional fence-sitter all my life, learning to bite my tongue when I've been dying to speak up. Show me a fence and I'll sit on it.' It is a skill that any President needs if he is to negotiate successfully with people from all political persuasions. When the Princess visits some of the countries where the regimes are totalitarian and, in some cases, absolute dictatorships, she is as charming and noncontroversial as any politician who is looking no further than the next vote. In her case, though, what she wants is for her charity to benefit, and if that means she has to act as if she is in total agreement with whoever she is talking to at that moment, so be it. She has acquired diplomatic skills that many would envy, even within her own family. Her ability to make friends with people with whom she obviously has little or nothing in common, either in background, upbringing or social standing, makes her a formidable candidate for the highest office if she so desired. As a Royal world traveller she has few equals. In 1995, she carried out 148 overseas engagements, with a further 427 at home. At the end of that year a national survey showed that her popularity had increased by 30 per cent.

When she faced the unhappiness of the breakdown of her first marriage, she did so without the need to bare all on television. There were no public battles, no confessions of adulterous

253

relationships, no angry recriminations—just a seamless transition to a second happy marriage.

The Princess Royal has no history of being involved with drugs, drink, financial scandal or unsuitable lovers. Skeletons in her cupboard seem to be remarkable by their absence. There are many politicians who would give their all to be able to say that, so what price President Anne in the twenty-first century?

CHAPTER SEVENTEEN

A FUTURE ROLE?

'I've always accepted the role of being second in everything from quite an early age . . . You start off in life very much a tail-end Charlie, at the end of the line.' These are the words of the Princess Royal in describing her position within the Royal Family and, in particular, in relation to her eldest brother, the Prince of Wales.

Psychologists have suggested many times that this feeling of inferiority is the main reason why Anne chose to marry commoners when she could have married into one of Europe's Royal families. By marrying Mark Phillips, an impecunious middle-class Army officer, and then Tim Laurence, who came from even further down the social scale, it is argued that she was reflecting how she saw her own status within the Royal circle.

For many years she was seen as the outsider in the Royal Family and she herself has acknowledged that she was the 'odd one out', a loner who found

254

herself being edged farther and farther from the centre as her two younger brothers came on to the scene and then even more so when the two sons of the Prince and Princess of Wales were born. In this she is like her father. He too has always regarded himself as being outside the inner circle, first of all because he is seen as a foreigner who just happened to marry the woman who became Queen, and later because, within the British constitution, there is no recognized role for the husband of a female Sovereign. He has been excluded from seeing all the State papers and official documents which arrive daily for the Queen's attention. In this he even takes a back seat to his eldest son, who does see some State papers, in preparation for the day when he becomes King.

So father and daughter have forged a natural closeness. In the early days of the Queen's reign, when Anne was still a child—she was only two years old when her mother became Queen—Prince Philip was the one who responded to his daughter's need for affection, as his wife struggled to master the complexities of a Queen Regnant. He has always appreciated Anne's qualities and understood why she has felt the need to prove herself as an individual, rather than merely as the daughter of the Queen. Prince Philip has done precisely the same thing himself, both in the public life of the nation and privately as a sportsman. So when Anne reached the highest levels in her chosen sport he was the first to congratulate her and to recognize why she had done it. They both knew that in the role of an aggressive and highly competitive world-class horsewoman, no one could ever accuse her of reaching the top because of her station in life or her Royal pedigree.

Her personality remains something of an enigma. She has inherited the characteristic of the 'Royal freeze' when she thinks someone has overstepped the mark, yet she can be the most spontaneous and informal of companions when the mood takes her. She has a caustic line in humour and her wit is rapier-sharp, to the point of hurtfulness on occasion. She is sharply intelligent, though no intellectual, and is clearly the most articulate and self-possessed member of her family.

It has not been easy for the Princess Royal to see two non-Royal women, Diana, Princess of Wales and the Duchess of York, enter the Royal scene and be acclaimed as the most popular women of their generation, although in the Duchess's case that particular situation was to alter dramatically in a very short time. If she felt any frustration at being pushed into the background by these newcomers, she disguised it well, and not by so much as a whisper has she let her feelings be known about their unconventional behaviour. Nevertheless, she has never pretended that the publicity that surrounds Diana's every move has not rankled with her. Having been through a separation and divorce herself with barely a ripple being caused either inside or outside the Royal Family, it would have been perfectly understandable if she had allowed herself some sort of satisfaction at the undignified public exhibitions of the Waleses and the Yorks as they fought their marital battles in the Press and on television. But if she ever did, no one could point to a single instance when she allowed her feelings or opinions to show.

In making her only daughter the Princess Royal,

the Queen solved a number of not too serious but slightly irritating family problems. When Prince Charles and, later, Prince Andrew married, their wives, taking their rank from their husband, enjoyed titles that were senior to that of Princess Anne even though she was the only one actually of Royal birth. The Queen was anxious for Anne to be recognized in her own right, and in bestowing what is one of the rarest of all titles—Anne is only the seventh Princess Royal since Charles I created the title for his daughter Princess Mary in 1642—Her Majesty elevated her to a special position within the Royal Family. The title is hers for life; it is not hereditary and it places her in a position where she does not have to rely on her husband, or anyone else, for her rank and style. It was a brilliant move on the part of the Queen, and even though the Princess is reluctant to discuss the matter, privately she is delighted and justifiably proud to hold such a distinguished and historic title.

When Prince Charles comes to the throne—and it is a question of when rather than if; there's no chance of him standing aside and allowing the succession to skip a generation—he will need a consort. As the likelihood is that he will remain single in order to make sure he gives no reason for dispute about his succession, the obvious person to stand beside him is his sister.

She has all the qualities which are important in that position: honesty, integrity, dignity and, above all, loyalty and total reliability. There would never be any chance of her letting him down. And nothing in her own private life has, or would, distract from her public performance. In over a quarter of a century of Royal duties she has never once given the slightest sign of boredom or of chafing at the never-ending, constant round of engagements. She believes passionately in the Monarchy and gets angry because she feels that if it is not to become an outdated and ridiculed institution, it has to move forward and be seen as a power for good.

Her knowledge and professionalism as a working Royal are unparalleled and she has achieved a place in the nation's life that is unique. By her own efforts she has transformed her image from that of an uncooperative, aggressive and spoilt young woman into a mature, hard-working and thoroughly dependable Princess whose devotion to duty is second to none. Nobody would be welcomed more by the people of the United Kingdom as consort to King Charles III. Of course, she would not stand beside him in Westminster Abbey to be crowned or have any official title. It would not be necessary for her to have that sort of recognition. She would simply act as the nation's hostess, and when it was felt essential for him to be accompanied by a woman, his sister would be there.

They would not share the responsibilities of Sovereignty in any constitutional manner. There would be no William and Mary situation or joint reign. But Anne is well versed in affairs of State, having been a Counsellor of State since 1971. She has acted on the Queen's behalf many times in that capacity during Her Majesty's absences abroad, and already knows a great deal about the day-to-day detail of Royal administration in relation to Government. She is also active as a stand-in monarch for the Queen, whom she has represented on a number of major overseas engagements.

An important development in the Princess Royal's ever-increasing public role within the Royal Family came in May 1996 when the Queen appointed her to be Lord High Commissioner of the Church in Scotland. This is the highest of all honours as the Lord High Commissioner takes up residence in the Palace of Holyroodhouse in Edinburgh during the General Assembly and is to all intents and purposes Sovereign for that week. The Princess held Court in the Scottish capital and it was later reported that she did so without once faltering. Was this then another step by Her Majesty in preparing her daughter for a future role?

Her experience would be invaluable to the Crown and to the country, and as her reputation throughout the Commonwealth has never been better, this move would also be welcomed in those countries where there might be certain reservations about Prince Charles reigning alone. She would be a priceless asset to the Monarchy, and her brother is well aware of this fact. One vital prerequisite for a successful monarch is self-confidence. The Queen has it in abundance. She has never for a moment doubted her ability to reign, and in the forty-five years she has been on the throne there has never been the slightest indication of any lack of belief in herself. None of the eleven Prime Ministers who have served her has ever had cause to question her authority; her very demeanour displays a natural regality and her decisiveness has become a byword among world leaders.

The Queen's father, King George VI, did not possess this same self-confidence when he first came to the throne. He was shy and nervous with a natural reserve that bordered on paranoia. His reluctance to accept the Crown has been well documented and the fact that he eventually became not only one of the best loved, but also one of the most successful Sovereigns this century, is said to be almost entirely due to the influence of his wife, the present Queen Mother. She had the 'spine of steel' any leader needs and it was she who instilled in her husband a belief in himself and in his ability to do the job.

The Prince of Wales will be the best prepared monarch Britain has ever seen when his turn to succeed eventually comes. But self-confidence does not come high on the list of his characteristics. He is not an arrogant man; self-pity is more the trait he shows most frequently. His father was never an affectionate parent, and since the death in 1979 of his honorary grandfather Lord Mountbatten, to whom he claimed to be able to say anything at all, there has been nobody to whom Charles can turn for support and advice. Prince Philip is either unable or unwilling to give Charles the guidance a son should be able to demand from an understanding father. It may not be all Prince Philip's fault. He has had enough problems of his own in coming to terms with his second-class citizen's role within the Royal Family, and as he has had to fight for himself every inch of the way to the position he now enjoys, he probably feels that his children should also be prepared to stand on their own two feet. Princess Anne has admitted that there was not a great deal of understanding or parental cosseting in their childhood. 'No one wanted to hear about your nerves. You just got on with it . . .'. It has even been suggested (by a certain malicious Royal 'insider') that another reason why the relationship between Prince Philip and Prince Charles has always been so strained is that Philip resents the fact that one day, if he outlives his wife, he will be required to bow his head to his own son.

Prince Charles has always been closer to his mother than to his father, but affectionate as she is, she is still Queen and the demands of the Monarchy take precedence in her mind over everything else—family included. What Charles obviously needs is someone who will give him the confidence in himself that his mother possesses. Again, that person could well be his sister, the Princess Royal. Her instinctive competitiveness on the sporting field and her natural aggression when dealing with bureaucracy, are exactly the features he will require to be a successful King, and she could be the one to give them to him.

Her old friend Andrew Parker Bowles, still one of her closest confidants, believes he has seen a remarkable change in the Princess Royal's character in the past twenty-five years. 'Once, when she was about twenty or twenty-one, I asked her what she would have liked to become if she had not been born Royal. She replied, "I could see myself as a PA to a leader of industry." Ask her that same question today and the answer would undoubtedly be that she would like to be that leader of industry. Nobody's assistant, but the boss. That's how her confidence has grown.'

The Princess has a quiet and determined concentration which remains undisturbed by outside influences, so she is able to separate her various roles into different compartments which rarely overlap. She has never had any problem in making up her mind. As her Private Secretary has said, the difficulty is getting her to change her mind once she's decided. Indecisiveness is not a word that enters her vocabulary. She may be wrong in some of the decisions she takes, but at least they are her own decisions and not based on the opinion of the last person she has spoken to, which has frequently been the case with the Prince of Wales.

If the Princess Royal became consort to her brother in all but name, she would bolster his confidence immensely. She believes he will be King and she knows he will be good at it. If there is anything at all she could do to assist him, she would willingly sacrifice the rest of her life in order to preserve the reputation of the Monarchy. In everything she does, or is asked to do, the number one question she asks is, 'Is it good for the Queen?' That has always been the overriding criterion when it comes to deciding which invitations to accept and which to decline. In this she shares a common cause with her father, who uses the same yardstick. So if it came to a question of forfeiting her own individual lifestyle—and she is recognized as the most independent of the Queen's children—in order to support her brother's role on the throne, there would be no contest. She would unhesitatingly forgo her own prime position as the most respected and hardworking member of the Royal Family to underpin Prince Charles. He needs someone like her, and as there is no one just like her, it would have to be her and no one else.

For years stories have circulated that Anne and Charles do not get on; that she tried to dominate him when they were children and that he resented her superiority at games. While it is true that as a youngster, Anne did outstrip her brother in physical pursuits, always getting the lion's share of pony rides and galloping when he was still trying to canter, as they grew older they developed a close and warm relationship. She refuses absolutely to criticize anything about Charles, and one of the things they share is their love of sport. Prince Charles has said that his favourite form of relaxation is 'doing something that completely exhausts me', and the Princess Royal feels the same way. She has boundless energy and only truly relaxes when she is engaged in some physically tiring activity.

While she was never trained in the way that Prince Charles has been trained practically from birth to become Sovereign, she has accumulated through her own efforts a vast store of knowledge and experience in world affairs. She has learnt to combine the early idealism of youth with the pragmatism that comes with practical experience gained over many years. After more than a quarter of a century of flawless public service she has become accepted as the most respected member of the Royal Family and, apart from her own mother and grandmother, perhaps also its most treasured.

The future of the 'Family Firm' may well depend on the one person who for so long was thought to be the odd one out. The Princess Royal could be the woman who will rescue the Monarchy, provide it with the strength it so badly needs, and see it safely into the twenty-first century.

APPENDIX I

HOLDERS OF THE TITLE
THE PRINCESS ROYAL

1 Princess Mary (1631–1660)
Daughter of Charles I

2 Princess Anne (1710–1759)
Daughter of George II

3 Princess Charlotte (1766–1828)
Daughter of George III

4 Princess Victoria (1840–1901)
Daughter of Queen Victoria

5 Princess Louise (1867–1931)
Daughter of Edward VII

6 Princess Mary (1897–1965)
Daughter of George V

7 Princess Anne (1950–)
Daughter of Elizabeth II